YO-CAX-536

Contents

SPIRIT OF THE B HIVE

'It's the 22-dollar suit of the clothing business; it's the hamburger of the butchers' shops; it's a seat in the bleachers. And there's a big market for all of them.' This was Nick Grinde's affectionate and ironic definition of the B movies, an industry in which the director of *White Bondage* (1937) and *Hitler — Dead or Alive* (1943) became a noted specialist.

Precisely what the B stood for is a matter of some debate — Bottom of the Bill, perhaps, or Bread and Butter, both terms unlikely to have bothered the hard-headed Grinde or the army of technicians and actors who between 1935 and the late 40s — the golden age of the B — turned out thousands of 70-minute second features. Unpretentious little films, for the most part, ideal for 'Duals' and 'Nabes' — double bills in neighbourhood theatres, in the crisp parlance of the time. Many of them still flicker away on late-night television: a youthful John Wayne rides again in Joseph Kane's *King of the Pecos*; an equally callow Robert Mitchum commits suicide in John Brahm's *The Locket*; a vivacious Louise Allbritton gives a low-budget performance worthy of Carole Lombard in Reginald LeBorg's *San Diego, I Love You*.

B movies have to be judged on their own terms, allowing for all the cruel exigencies which frequently dictated a dislocated and anarchic final form. Nevertheless, the very expression B movie conjures up images of creaking sets left over from half-forgotten epics, plots hanging in mid-air as time and money run out, aging stars stumbling through terrible indignities undreamt of in their heyday, wooden acting to rival the Petrified Forest in animation, and enough stock footage to wind several times round the Equator. Harsh lighting, perfunctory direction, sheer lack of interest, or of talent, and the sad ravages of time could on occasion lend added poignancy to William Beaudine's famous outburst, 'You mean somebody out there is actually waiting to see this?' Barton Maclane bellowing his laughable self-penned lines in *Man of Courage*; Bela Lugosi warily picking his way through *Mother Riley Meets the Vampire*, or literally dying on his feet in *Plan 9 from Outer Space*; a haggard Joan Crawford peremptorily written out of *I Saw What You Did*; Robert Taylor's features set in an immobile middle-aged mask in *The Nightwalker*; Steven Geray barely able to mutter his lines in *Jesse James Meets Frankenstein's Daughter*.

More endearing images of sheer tackiness linger in the mind with all the tenacity of a ball of chewing gum rammed on the underside of a table. At the end of *The Explosive Generation* Buzz Kulik's camera pulls back from William Shatner to reveal not only the microphone boom but also a tangled mass of wires and lights directly over the actor's head. Behind the looming crustacean monster in *The Gargan Terror,* one can glimpse a shadowy hand controlling its erratic movements. Confronted with The Fifty-Foot Woman, two doctors agree 'anything is possible in this jet-propelled age'.

If, however, the Bs were merely an embarrassing catalogue of meatheads doing their best — a kind of movie sub-species like the apes in *2001,* hopping about in the undergrowth at the base of the great standing stones of *Citizen Kane* or *Gone With the Wind* — they would long since have been cast into the dustbin of history, and along with them much of the work of such directors as Edgar Ulmer, Arthur Ripley, Robert Florey and Joseph H. Lewis. But the best low-budget films are made on talent not by spending money, a factor shared by the work of Edgar Ulmer at PRC in the 40s and the exploitation films made by Stephanie Rothman at New World in the 70s.

The B movie was a direct response by Hollywood to the falling cinema audiences of the early Depression years. Between 1930 and 1933 weekly attendances figures dropped from 110 million to 60 million. In an attempt to lure the audiences back the double bill was introduced. Where previously audiences had paid to see a single feature supplemented with shorts and cartoons, they were now treated to two features, one of which was a low-budget supporting film — the creature itself, the B.

In New York in October 1935 the two big theatre chains, RKO and Loew's (the holding company for MGM), adopted the double bill in all their principal theatres. This was a crucial moment in the development of the B movie industry, and within a year over 75 per cent of America's cinemas were running a double bill. However, with the Bs nothing is ever quite as simple as it seems. In the American South throughout the 30s and 40s, the single feature programme lingered on, and on Saturday night in many Southern cinemas the principal attraction was a B. There were two good reasons for this. The first lay in the nature of the audience — rural and unsophisticated — who naturally preferred a straightforward actioner starring Jack Holt or Richard Arlen to Lubitsch and Capra. The second reason is to be found in the system by which films were exhibited in the United States.

Until 1948 five major film studios — Warner Brothers, MGM, Paramount, Twentieth Century-Fox and RKO — owned the theatres in which their films were shown. In that year the Supreme Court, in an historic judgement delivered by Justice William O. Douglas, ruled that this convenient and immensely profitable arrangement violated the anti-trust laws, in the process hammering a substantial nail into the coffin of the B movie. Under the old arrangement the box office returns of an A feature were split between the exhibitor and distributor on a percentage basis, which varied according to the popularity of the film — the exhibitor's share might dip as low as ten per cent if the film was a big success. (For the five vertically integrated studios, this was perhaps a paper exercise, although the two sides of their business were always maintained under separate managements.) The Bs, on the other hand, were exhibited on a flat rental basis — hence the predilection of the Southern cinemas for second-feature fodder. With full houses and a relatively low rental they were in business. Nevertheless, under this system the major studios never lost money on a B. By the same token, the profits on individual second features were unlikely to steam up their accountants' pince-nez — on average a $10,000 profit on a B produced on a budget of $70-80,000.

All the major studios had their own B units, headed by men who knew every inch of the low-budget business: Sol C. Siegel at Paramount, Brian Foy at Warners, Lucien Hubbard and Michael Fessier at MGM, Irving Briskin at Columbia, and Ben Stoloff and Sol Wurtzel at Fox, the latter's name prompting the inevitable jibe, 'from bad to Wurtzel'.

Cordell Hickman and Billy Lee in *The Biscuit Eater.* Not all Bs were automatically destined for bottom-of-the-bill obscurity. This modest little Paramount film was voted among the National Board of Review's top ten films for 1940. Its immensely professional director Stuart Heisler shot this boy-and-dog story on location in Georgia, whose landscape was skilfully captured by cameraman Leo Tover.

Lloyd Nolan, with the knife-edge creases, gets tough with Roscoe Karns. A characteristically powerful Paramount line-up in the 1939 crime thriller *Tip-off Girls:* Larry Crabbe, Evelyn Brent, J. Carrol Naish and Anthony Quinn look on.

A crescendo of mild anxiety from Patric Knowles, C. Aubrey Smith and Lucille Ball as a less than optimistic Chester Morris attempts to restart their crashed aircraft. A great deal of talent went into the making of RKO's *Five Came Back* (1939). Dalton Trumbo wrote the screenplay from an original treatment by Nathanael West. John Farrow was the stylish director.

Understandably, the Bs from the majors reflected the studio's particular house styles. Warners, for example, recycled their 1930s G-Men movies into a series of efficient little Bs of the early 40s like *Bullets For O'Hara,* in the process using all the big action sequences from the originals. During the same period Paramount acquired a reputation for producing rather more enjoyable Bs than A features. Certainly, Robert Florey's 1938 *King of Alcatraz,* a breathtaking exercise in 58-minute economy, provided far more entertainment than many of the As it was designed to support, much of its flavour coming from its magnificent cast of Paramount character actors, including J. Carrol Naish, Lloyd Nolan, Robert Preston and Harry Carey.

During the 40s Paramount, with the aid of of the Pine-Thomas team, were able to maintain a steady stream of fast-paced action Bs. William Howard Pine had been an assistant to Cecil B. De Mille and William Thomas an associate producer of Bs at the Paramount studio. Their independent production team was set up with financial backing from Paramount. Their first release, in the spring of 1941, was *Power Dive,* with Richard Arlen and Jean Parker. It set a standard for straightforward outdoor action and wartime programmers whose titles — *Wildcat, Wrecking Crew, Torpedo Boat, Submarine Alert* — left little to the imagination. By 1945 they had produced 25 films, most of them directed by either Frank McDonald or William Berke. Richard Arlen and Jean Parker starred in eleven and the durable Chester Morris in eight.

A giant like MGM could afford to dress up its Bs more lavishly than most. Its impressive list of contract players, combined with the resources of a huge organization, resulted in a large number of polished Bs that could have passed for As elsewhere — a good example is provided by Edward L. Cahn's 1945 *Dangerous Partners,* with James Craig, Signe Hasso, Edmund Gwenn and Audrey Totter.

At the majors everyone was a contract, and the Bs provided an excellent method of absorbing overhead. But this was not the only function of these high-pressure workshops. They also provided a testing ground for promising young directors. In the early 30s William Wyler, a graduate of low-budget silent Westerns, was making cornball ZaSu Pitts comedies at Universal, while at the same studio George Stevens was directing *The Cohens and the Kellys in Trouble.* Edward Dmytryk served a long apprenticeship in the Bs, directing Lone Wolf and Boston Blackie features for Columbia, and *Captive Wild Woman* and *Hitler's Children* for RKO in 1943. Fred Zinnemann got his first break at MGM through Jack Chertok, then head of the shorts department (this was a familiar route to directing features which was also taken by Jacques Tourneur and Jules Dassin). He moved on quickly from *Kid Glove Killer* and *Eyes in the Night,* both made in 1942, to the prestigious *Seventh Cross.* Mark Robson and Robert Wise learnt their craft in Val Lewton's B unit at RKO. It's arguable that in a long career Robson never produced anything more satisfying than early efforts like the 1943 *Seventh Victim,* or *The Ghost Ship,* which he directed in the same year. In the mid-40s Anthony Mann worked on such diverse material as the low-budget RKO musical *The Bamboo Blonde,* and the noirish *Great Flamarion* with Erich von Stroheim and Mary Beth Hughes. On his arrival in America Robert Siodmak directed a number of interesting Bs, including *Fly By Night* (1942) and *Someone To Remember* (1943).

The B units also provided the studios with a handy tool with which to discipline recalcitrant leading men. In 1939 Humphrey Bogart found himself serving time in Warners' *King of the Underworld* as a 'moronic thug' in a reworking of an old Paul Muni vehicle, *Doctor Socrates.*

Young hopefuls were put through their paces in the Bs. Thus we find Richard Denning and Dennis Morgan in *King of Alcatraz:* Glenn Ford and Richard Conte in *Heaven With a Barbed Wire Fence* (1939 and directed

Paris on the PRC back lot. John Carradine as the murderer Gaston Morel in Edgar Ulmer's *Bluebeard* (1944).

MGM's *Kid Glove Killer* (1942) was a brief staging post on director Fred Zinnemann's route to better things. Van Heflin (left) played a police scientist unravelling a political murder. The film was produced by Jack Chertok who, as head of MGM's shorts department, had originated the 'Crime Does Not Pay' series, which gave several talents, including Zinnemann and Jules Dassin, their first chance.

Some directors spent a lifetime in the Bs. If they were master-craftsmen like Joseph H. Lewis, they could sometimes turn dross into gold. In *Lady Without a Passport* (1950) George Macready leans over to talk to Hedy Lamarr, one of a cargo of illegal immigrants he is smuggling from Havana into Florida. A hammered-down version of *Casablanca*, the film closes with desperate poignancy as the smuggler's plane – pursued by immigration cop John Hodiak – crashes into the Everglades, disgorging its hapless occupants not into the Promised Land but into a reeking swamp.

The series was one of the staples of the Bs.

top left
The gleam of perfect teeth; Christmas Carols sung by three Columbia starlets (l. to r.) Jinx Falkenburg, Evelyn Keyes and Marguerite Chapman, in a 1944 publicity shot. Falkenburg and Keyes were two of the nine young actresses crammed by producer Burt Kelly into that year's comedy-thriller *Nine Girls* directed by Leigh Jason.

top right
Lupe Velez oozing Latin-American charm all over Lyle Talbot in *Mexican Spitfire's Elephant* (RKO, 1942), one of the Mexican Spitfire series.

centre
The Red Dragon, a 1946 Monogram Charlie Chan adventure, directed by Phil Rosen, with the famed Oriental sleuth on the track of atom spies in Mexico City. Sidney Toler, wearing the weary look that characterized his later appearances as Chan, is sandwiched between Benson Fong (Number One Son) and Fortunio Bonanova.

left
And then there were the Saturday-afternoon thrills provided by serials. Ted Pearson gets his nose stuck while blazing away in Republic's *Dick Tracey's G-Men* (1939) starring Ralph Byrd.

by silent matinée idol Ricardo Cortez); Susan Hayward in Joseph Santley's *Sis Hopkins* (1941); and Jane Wyman in William Clemens' *Crime By Night* (1944). In Leigh Jason's 1944 *Nine Girls* for Columbia, the setting, a smart Californian girls' college, enabled the studio to use virtually all its contract ingenues at a stroke in a witty comedy-thriller. The ladies were Evelyn Keyes, Jinx Falkenburg, Anita Louise, Leslie Brooks, Lynn Merrick, Jeff Donnell, Nina Foch, Shirley Mills and Marcia Mae Jones.

The Bs could also provide a relatively dignified rest home for stars whose careers were on the slide: Warner Baxter ended his days with Columbia's Crime Doctor series; Richard Arlen found a regular berth in the Pine-Thomas actioners of the 40s and early 50s; Richard Dix signed off with the 'Whistler' films for Columbia.

Performers like Tom Conway, Tom Neal, Chester Morris, Jane Frazee and Louise Allbritton never threw off the B tag, but given the right chemistry they could find themselves working on a project displaying a rare order of talent. In RKO's 1939 *Five Came Back,* Chester Morris starred alongside Lucille Ball, Wendy Barrie, John Carradine, Patric Knowles and C. Aubrey Smith. The script was drafted by Nathanael West and completed by Dalton Trumbo, and the stylish direction was by John Farrow.

While ambitious young directors and actors in the majors nursed dreams of the big time, at the independents even bigger dreams were built on even smaller budgets. Perhaps the true story of the Bs is to be found here, in the rented studios, skimpy standing sets and occasionally inspired improvizations of 'poverty row'. The early 30s saw the rapid growth and equally rapid disappearance of a number of small independent studios, their birth, death or absorption into a marginally bigger unit resembling one of those speeded-up medical films in which milling blood cells attempt to repel an invading virus. Tiffany (Tiffany-Stahl in the silent era), a prolific but short lived producer of Ken Maynard Westerns, was taken over in 1932 by Sono Art-World Wide, shortly before both disappeared forever into the hungry maw of Twentieth Century-Fox. By 1936 ambitious but undercapitalized outfits like Chesterfield, Invincible, Mayfair and Majestic had all gone into liquidation. Three years later the survival of the fittest had left behind Monogram, Republic and Grand National, the last going under in the same year after its head, Edward Alperson, had invested nearly a million dollars in a musical turkey, *Something to Sing About,* which in the event proved to be something to weep about. From the wreckage of Grand National emerged the most fascinating B phenomenon of the 40s, Producers Releasing Corporation, which was headed by a former film exchange manager, Ben Judell.

Monogram was founded in the 1920s by Ray Johnston and Trem Carr — it went through several changes of name, including Rayart, before emerging as Monogram. The studio had a truly beautiful logo which instantly evokes the flavour of the period: a streamliner train emerging from a tunnel pulling behind it Monogram Pictures in Art Deco lettering. In keeping with this bold image some of Monogram's early efforts made a bid for the quality market with adaptations of *Oliver Twist, Black Beauty* and *The Moonstone.* But like all small studios Monogram found it all but impossible to land a big name; in lieu of Warners' gangster star James Cagney, they had to make do with his younger brother William in a number of undistinguished thrillers.

At the end of 1934 Johnston and Carr ran foul of Herbert Yates, the head of Consolidated Film Laboratories, a film-processing company that handled many B features. Yates had decided to become a movie mogul, and he accomplished this by the simple but ruthless method of foreclosing on and taking over Monogram and Mascot (a serial factory), both of which were heavily in debt to his film lab. The result was the Republic studio. Nat

Levine, who had headed Mascot at the time of the take over, stayed with Yates to launch a stream of serials which became one of Republic's staples. But for the independent-minded Johnston and Carr the honeymoon was inevitably brief after such a shotgun marriage. Within two years they had left Republic and revived Monogram.

Monogram's speciality was the series film — Charlie Chan, East Side Kids, Mr Wong (with Boris Karloff), Bomba the Jungle Boy, Rough Riders and Cisco Kid — although they never dabbled in serials. Scott R. Dunlap, an extremely able producer, was often given the task of establishing a new series' reputation. Once his task was accomplished, the budgets and the quality took an inevitable nose dive while the series coasted along on the strength of its initial impact.

Monogram also used enterprising independent producers like Sam Katzman, whose Banner Pictures — a kind of Monogram B unit, if there could be such a thing — produced a number of rock-bottom horror films starring Bela Lugosi. The tone was set by *Spooks Run Wild* in which the studio's East Side Kids encounter Dracula, a sad indication of the depths to which Lugosi had fallen since his triumphs of the early 30s.

The King brothers (Maurice, Herman and Frank Kozinski), three movie-struck businessmen who muscled in on Hollywood in the early 40s, produced a number of excellent thrillers for Monogram. Unsophisticated, sometimes downright rude, they nevertheless had a tremendous flair for producing profitable little B movies. Memorable among their output was the 1944 *When Strangers Marry*, directed by William Castle, starring Kim Hunter, Dean Jagger and Robert Mitchum, and with Rhonda Fleming in her first screen role; the score was written by Dimitri Tiomkin. The total cost to Monogram came in at well under $50,000.

Monogram did not own any theatres (of the independents only PRC was in this position) and in the 30s relied on the states rights system of distribution. This enabled the independents to farm out the distribution of their product on a territorial basis. During this period this operation was handled for Monogram by First Division, which also distributed Chesterfield and Invincible films. In time both Monogram and Republic set up film exchanges of their own in America's big cities, but the other independents continued to use their franchisees in Atlanta, Chicago and elsewhere. In the 1970s Roger Corman's New World Pictures was still using this convenient system — it involved no outlay beyond the franchisee's percentage of the film's profits.

In November 1945, Steve Broidy, Monogram's aggressive sales manager, replaced Johnston as the studio's president. In an attempt to move upmarket Monogram began to release a number of more generously budgeted productions under the Allied Artists label, a wholly owned subsidiary. For a while the old Monogram B factory and Allied Artists existed side by side. During the time director Phil Karlson took to make the Allied Artists *Black Gold* (1947), with Anthony Quinn and Katherine De Mille, he also completed four characteristic Monogram cheapies, including a Gale Storm musical and a Charlie Chan adventure.

Six years later the Monogram name was dropped altogether, and under Steve Broidy Allied Artists went on to produce such commercial and critical successes as Billy Wilder's *Love in the Afternoon* and William Wyler's *Friendly Persuasion*, while still financing such low-budget classics as Roger Corman's 1958 *War of the Satellites*. In 1960 Jean-Luc Godard provided a timely reminder of the affection in which the old studio was still held by dedicating his first feature, *Breathless*, to Monogram.

PRC had a brief six-year life before being absorbed by Eagle-Lion, an offshoot of British flour magnate J. Arthur Rank's film empire. In 1951, in a now familiar process, Eagle-Lion was swallowed up by United Artists.

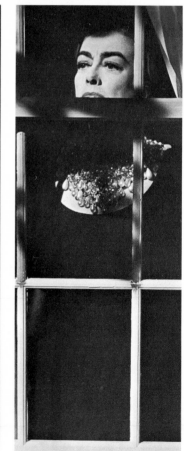

The twilight of three careers and the beginning of three others.

top left
Erich von Stroheim and Edward Van Sloan in *The Mask of Dijon* (PRC, 1946), a melodrama about a homicidal magician played by von Stroheim. Despite its miniscule budget, it displays an intermittent visual flair which suggests that journeyman director Lew Landers took a few tips from the master.

bottom far left
Bela Lugosi slumming it with the East Side Kids in Monogram's 1941 *Spooks Run Wild.* Huntz Hall has his hands on his hips, Leo Gorcey seems to be brandishing a skull and Sunshine Sammy Morrison is leaning over the bannister.

bottom left
Joan Crawford, wearing a medium-size chandelier round her neck, in William Castle's low-budget psychological thriller *I Saw What You Did* (1965). She is about to be knifed by boyfriend John Ireland.

top right
Jane Wyman and an invisible Jeffrey Lynn in D. Ross Lederman's light-hearted *The Body Disappears* (1941). Lynn has been made invisible by professor Edward Everett Horton's experimental life-preserving serum.

centre right
Lionel Barrymore, Van Johnson and George Read watch a lovely Ava Gardner try to put it over on a gas station attendant in MGM's *Three Men in White* (1944), a Dr Gillespie film directed by Willis Goldbeck. The series format provided a convenient vehicle for the introduction of promising young actors like Johnson and Gardner.

bottom right
A youthful Jack Nicholson in Roger Corman's *The Terror,* (1963), the quickest of that irreverent and inventive director's quickies. Clips from *The Terror* played a significant part in Peter Bogdanovich's first film, *Targets* (1968).

right
A staple of the traditional B thriller was the cynical, trench-coated cop. You can tell by the way Charles McGraw is smoking his cigarette that he is from this hard-boiled school in Richard Fleischer's taut *The Narrow Margin* (RKO, 1952).

below left
King of the Cowboys Roy Rogers closes the book on Dale Evans and the slightly apprehensive Sons of the Pioneers in a production number from Republic's 1944 *Song of Nevada*, directed by Joseph Kane.

below right
Into the 50s, with Maria Corday stylishly threatened by a well-groomed giant spider's claw in Universal's 1955 *Tarantula*, one of the best of the 'insect invasion' cycle, directed by Jack Arnold.

left
Undercover narcotics agent Russ Tamblyn is struck dumb by the remarkable physique of his 'aunt' Mamie Van Doren in Jack Arnold's *High School Confidential* (1958). Jan Sterling seems less impressed. Producer Albert Zugsmith took over as director in 1960 for *College Confidential* and *Sex Kittens Go to College*, in which Mamie plays a stripper with a genius IQ who is chosen to head a college science department.

below left
A peroxide Mamie Van Doren look-alike in *She Demons*, a 1958 schlock classic. Shipwrecked with her companions on an island which is shortly to become a Navy bomb target and is infested with whip-wielding Nazis, she can only bleat plaintively 'Where's my powder blue cashmere shortie?'

above
Duckboards provide a charming example of the period's concept of space travel. In the 50s British producers attempted to give their films a little extra gloss by importing second-rank American stars. In 1955 Brian Donlevy was hired by Hammer to play Dr Bernard Quatermass in *The Quatermass Experiment*, adapted from Nigel Kneale's television series. With assistant Maurice Kaufmann he is examining a space probe which has returned with all its crew missing except one.

During the 40s PRC ran hard to keep up with Monogram and Republic, but many of their offerings hovered closer to the 'Z' rather than the B category. Dreadful George Zucco horror vehicles like *The Mad Monster* or such unintentionally hilarious wartime spy melodramas as *Miss V from Moscow,* with Lola Lane, shrieked 'poverty row' from every frame. Nevertheless, from 1942-46, PRC provided a home for 'poverty row' patron saint, Edgar Ulmer, whose bleak little 1946 road movie, *Detour* — a two-hander with Tom Neal, Ann Savage, a single set and a back-projection machine — was one of the best, and most cheaply made, of all B movies.

Brilliant directors like Zinnemann could vault quickly from the B production line to the sunny uplands of prestige productions. Many more stayed behind, their sheer efficiency at grinding out a film in as little as four days condemning them to a lifetime in second features. In 1942 Lew Landers made thirteen films for Columbia, ranging from *The Boogie Man Will Get You* (a reworking of *Arsenic and Old Lace*) to *Alias Boston Blackie.* In the same year William Beaudine directed six films for PRC, including the excellent *Panther's Claw,* and four for Monogram. In 1948, when time was running out for the Bs, Beaudine completed nine films for Monogram, among them a tight little thriller typical of the period, *Incident,* with Jane Frazee and Warren Douglas. Sam Newfield, a PRC workhorse who directed twelve Westerns in 1941, was so prolific that it was necessary for him to use two pseudonyms, 'Sherman Scott' and 'Peter Stewart'.

For the independents, speed was of the essence. Even in Monogram's best year, 1947, the flat rental system restricted the studio to an average profit per film (they released 29), of just under $13,000. In a bad year, an extra day's shooting on a film could wipe out its paper-thin margin. Directors were seldom allowed the luxury of second thoughts. As Reginald LeBorg told me, 'What Hitchcock did in three to six months of preparation — namely having every shot of the whole picture designed with the help of the art director — the B movie director had to do in his head, with only a week or two of preparation.'

Paradoxically, the apparently insuperable limitations imposed by the independents could give a director a degree of freedom which did not exist in the B units of the majors, or at Universal and Columbia, all of which tended to reflect the hierarchical nature of A productions. Edgar Ulmer, reluctant to be 'ground up in the Hollywood hash machine', was able to conjure films from thin air at PRC. *Isle of Forgotten Sins* was created around a handy miniature of 200 palm trees left over from John Ford's *The Hurricane. Club Havana,* a ludicrously cheap version of *Grand Hotel,* was improvised from a one-page outline and shot on a single set. *Girls in Chains,* shot in five days, was developed from a newspaper headline about a scandal in a women's prison — an approach which forshadowed the New World exploitation films of the 70s. In an interview with Peter Bogdanovich in 1970, Ulmer remarked of PRC, 'It was a nice family feeling, not too much interference; if there was interference, it was only that we had no money, that was all.'

There was no item of expenditure, however small, that could be allowed to escape a B director's attention. In the 40s a character with a non-speaking part — a bell boy, for example, taking the hero's suitcase up to his room — earned $16.50 a day. If he opened his mouth to say 'Yes Sir', the fee automatically went up to $25. No matter how much business the bell boy might have, someone could always be relied on to come up with a ploy to save the vital eight-fifty — perhaps he might have laryngitis and have to write his replies on a slip of paper, a ruse recalled by Nick Grinde in an article written in 1946.

At the same time a B producer might beg, borrow or steal a big standing set from a more lavish production. Universal used the big sets from the 1931 *Frankenstein* in *Flash Gordon* (1936), and the master-set from *Green Hell* in

Sometimes the Bs attempted exposés of social problems, the exercise invariably being accompanied by some fairly imaginative publicity.

Unwed mother Meg Randall is congratulated for her part in smashing an illegal baby adoption racket by District Attorney Jeff Chandler, Gale Storm and newspaperman Dennis O'Keefe in *Abandoned* (Universal, 1949).

far left
William Castle's *It's a Small World* (1950) chronicled the adventures of a midget and his fight through to success and romance.

left
A strained Scott Brady and Mona Freeman with their backs to the wall in Charles Lamont's *I Was a Shoplifter* (1950), in which an underworld gang blackmails kleptomaniacs into going to work for them.

Yvonne Buckingham as Christine Keeler, the woman at the heart of Britain's biggest post-war political scandal, in an exploitation quickie *The Christine Keeler Story*. The man on the extreme right seems to be enjoying himself.

The Mummy's Hand (1940) plus a good deal of convenient flashback footage from the original 1932 Karloff film. RKO's *The Master Race* (1944) marches the British army through a wartorn northern European town which in reality is a slightly dishevelled section of the medieval Parisian streets erected for *The Hunchback of Nôtre Dame*. RKO also never passed up an opportunity to make use of the enormous set built for Orson Welles' *The Magnificent Ambersons,* and it provided the atmospheric apartment house in *Cat People*. The budget-conscious Pine-Thomas team were adept at searching out economic locations for their action films. The 1943 *Aerial Gunner* was filmed at a US government gunnery school, both cutting costs and adding authenticity to the picture.

One of the *leitmotifs* of the Bs was the liberal use of library footage, particularly for big action sequences, out of the question on a B budget. If you had missed Wesley Ruggles' action-packed RKO Western *Cimarron* when it was released in 1930, a regular diet of the studio's subsequent oaters would have provided you with all of its best moments. Serial producers plundered the library shelves with gay abandon. The 1954 Columbia serial *Riding with Buffalo Bill* dressed its leading man, William Marshall, in the same costume as the 1940 serial hero Deadwood Dick, enabling all the action sequences from the earlier epic to be trundled out again. Examples of the more interesting and outrageous uses of stock footage will be found throughout the book. In the Bs they were legion.

If the sets and much of the action had a distinctly familiar look about them, so did the plots. Perhaps this is a slightly unfair charge to level at the Bs, as Hollywood has always been a creature which has thrived by devouring its own progeny and then spewing them up again still in recognizable form. At Fox writers on both As and Bs laboured to twist storylines into versions of the half dozen or so plotlines beloved of studio boss Darryl F. Zanuck. Nevertheless, in the B units writers were left in little doubt as to what was required of them. Warners B-man Brian Foy would brusquely instruct hacks stumped for a story to rewrite Howard Hawks' 1932 *Tiger Shark* (two men, one young, one old in love with the same woman). In Hawks film the two protagonists were tuna fishermen, but for the purposes of a B they could follow any profession, preferably more glamorous and with an element of danger. Barton Maclane, a stalwart of Warner B actioners, got the *Tiger Shark* treatment in *Bengal Tiger* in 1936. When they were not tinkering with *Tiger Shark*, Foy's writers were ploughing their way through a towering pile of scripts stacked up by his desk. As soon as a film was wrapped up, the script was returned to the bottom of the pile. A new writer was handed the one on the top and told to change its background.

At PRC in the 40s, Edgar Ulmer, Leon Fromkess and Sigmund Neufeld would start the season by dreaming up about fifty titles. As Ulmer put it, 'the stories had to be written to fit the cockeyed titles'. At Columbia the titles of Bs yet to be made were posted on a large blackboard, waiting for new writers to give them a ten-page treatment. If the treatment was approved, the script was completed and the film was made.

A good storyline is seldom allowed to go to waste. Rudolf Maté's *D.O.A.,* one of the most interesting of postwar films noir, was remade in 1969 as *Colour Me Dead. The Petrified Forest* turned up in 1945 as *Escape in the Desert,* with Nazi Helmut Dantine in the Bogart role. *Eve Knew Her Apples* (1945), was a musical variation of *It Happened One Night; Cape Town Affair* (1967), a leaden remake of Sam Fuller's 1953 *Pickup on South Street,* this time with a South African setting. The 1958 Audie Murphy vehicle, *Gun Runners,* was the remake of *To Have and Have Not.* Stuart Heisler's *I Died a Thousand Times,* with Jack Palance and Shelley Winters, is an inferior version of *High Sierra. Tension* (1949), with Audrey Totter at her most viperish, is straight out of the school of *Double Indemnity*. Interestingly, Edgar Ulmer was sufficiently emboldened by the success of Billy Wilder's film to suggest that PRC rush out a rip-off version entitled *Single Indemnity*. The film was made, but, alas, with a different title.

At the end of February 1953 the last act of the divestiture drama took place when the Warner Brothers theatre chain was acquired by the Stanley Warner Corporation. It coincided with the death throes of the B movie in its classical form. Weekly cinema attendance figures were again on the slide after achieving an all-time high during the Second World War, when escape-hungry audiences constituted nearly 70 per cent of the total population of the US. By 1957 the figures had slumped from this peak of 100 million to 40 million, well on the way to the 20 million of the early 70s.

It remained for television to deliver the *coup de grâce*, providing a stream of 30-minute Westerns and thrillers which effectively undercut the lingering appeal of the cinema second feature. There was simply no future in such Republic staples as the $50,000 'Jubilee budget' Westerns when the public could watch similar fare on the small screen. Ironically, *Rawhide, Laramie* and *Cheyenne* were produced by the very men who had laboured so long on the B production lines. Directors like Lesley Selander, Joseph Kane and Lew Landers moved easily from the tight schedule of the Bs to the even tighter schedules of television. As a television executive told me, 'When we had a picture we wanted finished in two days, we called in someone like Lew Landers. He was like sugar and flour in a grocery store — unexciting but always reliable.' At the same time a number of leading men from Bs of the late 40s and early 50s — Guy Madison, William Lundigan, Grant Williams and Craig Stevens — also made the transition to television, starring in their own series.

In the 60s television provided an echo of the old B format with the 'made for TV film', a tag which produces a sinking of the heart in any discriminating viewer. Just like the old flat-rental Bs, their makers have a clear idea of the slot into which they will fit and of the revenue which they can expect from them. Inevitably, formulaic plotting, low-budget copies of current cinema fads, and a collection of fading stars and young hopefuls have created great arid tracts of television time, a kind of media equivalent of the Dustbowl. In the 50s second-rank American leading men whose careers were on the slide like Forrest Tucker, Zachary Scott and Brian Donlevy, went to Britain to make feeble thrillers. Even Ronald Reagan got the star treatment. Nowadays their successors end up in 'made for TV' films. The results are usually the same.

One example will suffice. *Katie, Portrait of a Centrefold*, like many of the sexploitation movies of the 40s, flatters to titillate, and in the end delivers very little. The plot is as old as the hills, as starry-eyed Katie wins a local beauty contest in Benson, Texas (hosted by a spectral Fabian), and sets off for Hollywood and a career in modelling. Needless to say the hapless little thing is ripped off by everyone in sight, including stars of yesteryear Tab Hunter and Dorothy Malone. The film makes a flabby attempt to expose the 'ruthless world' of modelling, but its limping direction and wooden performances serve to endorse the fatuous values it is trying to savage. However, there is one cherishable moment. When disillusioned Katy returns home, she is taken to task by her aunt/guardian: 'It's hard for your uncle Hank, what with your nekkid picture on every barn door for 20 miles'.

From the early 50s the B movie entered a new phase, that of the cheaply made exploitation picture. The process of divestiture had opened up fresh possibilities for independent producers. Although cinema attendance figures were falling, there were clearly identifiable areas for which the majors were not catering, principally the drive-in cinemas with their predominantly teenage audiences. It only remained for America to

An early, and somewhat crude, Roger Corman role reversal movie. Marie Windsor threatens Michael 'Touch' Connors in the 1956 *Swamp Women*.

A little bit of sex and a little bit of violence: The New World style in Jonathan Kaplan's *Student Teachers* (1973).

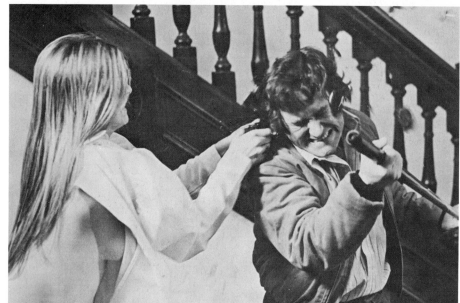

'We like it violent, violent, violent!' Paul Bartel's *Death Race 2000* (1975).

Super-cool Peter Fonda observes Bruce Dern's wake in *Wild Angels* (1966), Roger Corman's revival of the bike movie.

Tidal Wave, a Japanese disaster movie bought by New World in 1973. Corman threw out everything except the special effects and then added additional footage with Lorne Greene playing an American UN delegate explaining why the world was being swamped by a monster wave. Critical reaction to this effort was mixed.

discover teenagers, and that was not long in coming. Into the gap stepped a number of enterprising entrepreneurs: grizzled veterans of the old B units, William Castle and Sam Katzman (who had turned Johnny Weissmuller into Jungle Jim when he became too old for Tarzan); Albert Zugsmith, who had produced Orson Welles' *Touch of Evil* at MGM; Samuel Z. Arkoff and James Nicholson, founders of American International Pictures (AIP) in 1955; and Roger Corman, a prolific producer-director and the man whose name is most closely associated with the exploitation films of the last 25 years.

They grasped that changing patterns of distribution, falling audiences, and the sheer cost of colour film, had killed off the old-style second feature. There was little point in attempting to set up a 50s version of Monogram, supplying a market that no longer existed. Instead, they created a market of their own with low-budget, original films which, however crudely, mirrored the changing face of America, and particularly of teen America. What they lacked in production values, or even comprehensibility, they made up for with Mamie Van Doren and Fay Spain.

Just as the B thrillers of the late 40s recall the dark side of postwar urban America — none more powerfully than Joseph H. Lewis' *Gun Crazy* (1949) — so the Zugsmith-Arkoff-Katzman exploitation cycle enshrines all the teen torment of the late 50s. The best of them — *Teenage Doll, High School Confidential, Date Bait* — possessed a sufficiently outrageous self-confidence to become an instant part of the 'kid-kulture' from which they sprang. Others, like Sam Katzman's frantic *Mamboo Boom*, or the later *Miniskirt Mob*, are sufficiently wide of the mark to provide surreal reminders of dance fads and fashion crazes of the past, no doubt ripe for revival in the not-too-distant future. I vividly recall trekking one winter evening to watch an all-night show of Alan Freed rock'n'roll nonsense at the Scala cinema, London, only to find my way barred by serried ranks of sixteen-year-old versions of Eddie Cochrane and Ritchie Valens whose studied recreations of these old heroes' styles seemed more authentic than anything that subsequently appeared on the screen. Sadly, none of them seemed to recognize Eddie when he appeared in *Untamed Youth*. All eyes were on Mamie Van Doren's interesting physique.

Science fiction and horror cheapies, often with a 'wild youth' twist (*Teenage Caveman, I Was a Teenage Werewolf, Teenage Zombies, Teenagers from Outer Space*), dragsters versus bikers (*Dragstrip Riot, Hot Car Girl*), the demon marijuana (*High School Confidential, Wild Youth, Date Bait*) and the endless beach party (*Bikini Beach, How to Stuff a Wild Bikini*), were all interchangeable elements in the exploitation game, providing the raw material for drive-in programmes featuring a combination bill. AIP were expert at preparing these packages, their first in 1956 pairing Roger Corman's *The Day the World Ended* with *Phantom from 10,000 Leagues*.

The budgets on these classics of social realism seldom exceeded $100,000, with just as much spend on promotion. Joe Levine, who made a fortune by acquiring the distributions rights to the muscleman epic *Hercules* in 1959, never tired of reminding everyone that he was in a 'circus business', and the biggest three-ring circus of them all was run by the tireless showman William Castle. Castle, who loved to introduce his films in the Hitchcock manner, specialized in psychological thrillers beefed up with aging stars (*The Nightwalker* with Robert Taylor and Barbara Stanwyck; *I Saw What You Did* with Joan Crawford and John Ireland) and novelty horror films (*The Tingler, House on the Haunted Hill*, with Vincent Price). No gimmick was too farfetched to sell these films — life insurance policies against the unlikely possibility of members of the audience succumbing to heart attacks brought on by the feeble plot twists and special effects; sections of the cinema seating fitted with seat belts to prevent you jumping out of your skin; skeletons winging their way across the auditorium in Castle's fabulous 'Emergo' process; and seats electrically wired to give your back a little frisson when the Tingler got loose in the audience.

Roger Corman's New World Pictures was still working hard at it in the 70s. In 1975 his sales manager reckoned that up 'to 70 per cent of any exploiter's initial biz lies in the title and campaign'. The copyline for the 1972 *Big Bird Cage* — a women's prison picture in the grand tradition of *Women in Chains* — ran, 'Women so hot with desire they melt the chains that enslave them.' *Fly Me*, a quickie made in the Philippines and released by New World in 1973, invited the public to 'See stewardesses battle kung fu killers.' For *Piranha*, a characteristic New World combination of *Jaws* rip-off and old-fashioned monster-on-the-loose shocker, exhibitors were urged to 'Tie in the local fish store and arrange for a piranha-filled aquarium to be placed in your lobby. Scattering a few old rings and watches on the bottom should complete the effect.'

New World produced the most consistently successful exploitation films of the 70s. Formed in 1970 after Corman became dissatisfied with the re-editing of *Gas-s-s-s* by AIP, New World became a focus for bright young film makers, eager to break into the guild-controlled movie industry. As a producer Corman's ability to encourage, or exploit, promising directors is legendary. (Paul Bartel received a fee of $3,500 for directing the immensely successful *Death Race 2000.*)Francis Ford Coppola (*Dementia 13*, 1963), Peter Bogdanovich (*Targets*, 1968) and Martin Scorsese (*Boxcar Bertha*, 1972) have all passed through his hands. In true PRC style, *Targets* was built around day's work which Boris Karloff owed Corman. The drive-in cinema where the film reaches its climax is showing *The Terror*, which was improvized by Corman when *The Raven* was completed two days inside schedule. These brisk lessons in economy seem to have been forgotten by the Young Turks of the cinema in their subsequent careers.

New World films are full of jokey references to Corman's low-budget triumphs of the past. The carnivorous plant from *The Little Shop of Horrors* turns up behind a locked cell door in *Eat My Dust*, still plaintively crying 'Feed Me!' In 1976 New World even produced an amusing tribute to itself. Joe Dante and Allan Arkush's *Hollywood Boulevard* was the result of a bet by Jon Davison, New World's publicity head, that he could make a movie for at least one third of New World's previous cheapest, *Student Nurses*, which cost $120,000. (Corman jumped at the wager but cannily limited the budget to $60,000.) The result was a freewheeling in-house joke about two starlets — Candy Rialson and Mary Woronov, New World's famous 'tits 'n' terror' duo — working for a low-budget film company. The action is lashed together with miles of New World stock footage, guest appearances by Godzilla and the Fly, and a sardonic running commentary by Corman veteran Dick Miller as an agent with a line in weird clients.

Corman has now relinquished his role as a director and has personally produced only one New World film, Monte Hellman's 1974 *Born to Kill*, which, ironically, was the last New World film to lose money. Nevertheless the company's product bears Corman's stamp and reflects his keen grasp of the changing tastes of his predominantly American audiences. His sureness of touch has rarely deserted him. Although New World released several black exploitation ('blaxploitation') films in the early 70s — *The Final Comedown*, *Savage* and *Darktown Strutters* — Corman sensibly hung back from the scramble that was developing for a market catering for only ten per cent of the population of the United States and an even smaller percentage overseas. Early in 1977 he told an interviewer: 'The last couple of years I thought that a large proportion of the public wanted to see blood or breasts. Now I think they want to see cars. Our biggest film to date, *Eat My Dust*, just piles up one car after another.'

Scripts were closely vetted by Corman, who then gave his directors an overall framework within which to work. Jonathan Kaplan, director of *Night Call Nurses*, recalls that Corman's succinct list of requirements for the film — the result of a ten-minute meeting — were as follows: the exploitation of male sexual fantasies; plenty of action and violence; two subplots, one comic and the other reflecting liberal, left-of-centre values. Then a little more advice: frontal nudity from the waist up; total nudity from behind; absolutely no pubic hair; and the exploitation of the title within the film.

This kind of calculation has enabled New World to develop several areas of activity. First, Corman has mined the classic exploitation seam, producing films which imitate or pre-empt the big projects of the major studios. The most successful, Paul Bartel's *Death Race 2000*, was vastly more enjoyable than its lumbering progeniter, *Rollerball*, and, despite its ragged edges, achieved a degree of audience manipulation which at times was worthy of Hitchcock. Corman has also revisited familiar territory with biker movies (*Angels Die Hard!*) and a revival of Jack Arnold's monster-on-the-loose cycle of the 50s, often with a trendy ecological gloss, as in *Humanoids from the Deep*. There are ecological undercurrents (the evils of strip mining) running through *Fighting Mad*, produced by Corman for Fox in 1976, one of the number of revenge melodramas which fed off the success of Phil Karlson's 1973 *Walking Tall*. Finally there was the development of the role reversal theme with which Corman himself had dabbled in the early 50s in *Swamp Women*, *Viking Women and the Sea Serpent* and *Gunslinger*.

Two distinct strands emerged: the 'nurse' cycle, which was prompted by the success of Stephanie Rothman's *Student Nurses*, and the women's prison series, the first of which was *The Big Doll House*, shot in the Philippines by Jack Hill. The strands came together in *The Hot Box* (1972) in which a group of American nurses working in a banana republic are captured by a band of revolutionaries. These films highlight the contradictory elements which often tug away at each other in New World product of the early 70s. The placing of assertive, independent women at the centre of the stage, but in a context which seems aimed at fuelling male fantasies of torture and lesbianism; and the uneasy blending of a liberal, political viewpoint with the crude stereotypes and plot conventions of the exploitation format. It is a tribute to the skill of directors like Stephanie Rothman and Barbara Peeters (whose *Bury Me An Angel* has a tough, revenge-obsessed biker heroine) that, saddled with these limitations, they can still produce work which is informed with feminist ideas. Even with films like *The Great Texas Dynamite Chase* — a thinly disguised version of *Butch Cassidy and the Sundance Kid* — the effect can be both amusing and subversive. At one point bank robbers Claudia Jennings and Jocelyn Jones are held at gunpoint by a randy highway patrol man with just one thing on his mind. Almost before he knows it, the poor fool find himself chained to a tree with his pants down by his ankles and a fizzing stick of dynamite between his feet. In keeping with the good-natured radicalism of the film, he is not blown to bits. Embarrassment and humiliation (so often visited on women in exploitation pictures) is his punishment. Perhaps Corman himself should have the last world. Of *The Big Bird Cage*, he said, 'It was the story of women in prison, with a little bit of sex, a little bit of violence and a *great deal* of humour.'

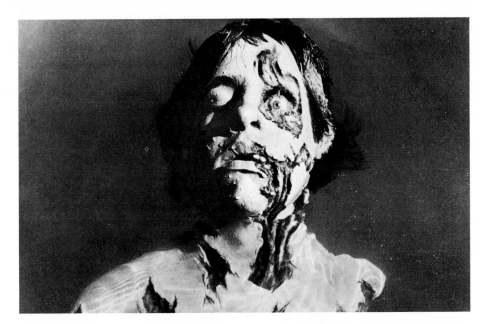

The sad result of a brief encounter with a killer fish in Joe Dante's *Piranha* (1977). A New World promotion shot aimed at exhibitors urged, 'Promote community interest and fear by organizing groups (Boy Scouts, citizen volunteers) to guard against the "coming onslaught". Give enterprising kids in your area a few bucks to make themselves scarce for a few days. Watch your grosses soar.'

Unclassifiable, unspeakable, a minor kitsch masterpiece. Joseph E. Levine's no-expenses-spared space epic *Santa Claus Conquers the Martians* (1964).

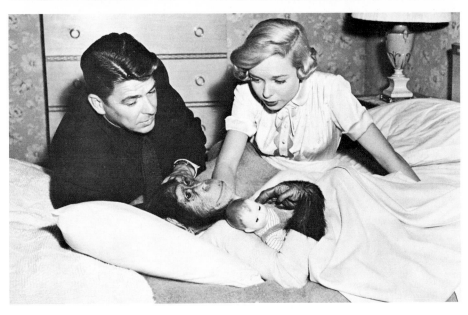

Ronald Reagan, Diana Lynn and Bonzo in Frederick de Cordova's *Bedtime for Bonzo* (1951), one of the many thankless B efforts through which the future president struggled gamely in the 1950s.

27

MY GUN IS QUICK
THRILLERS

'I wanna report a murder — mine,' croaks Edmond O'Brien as he staggers into a Los Angeles police station at the beginning of Rudolph Maté's *D.O.A.* Kicking off with one of the great opening lines in B-movie history, the inevitable flashback takes a vertiginous plunge into the nightmare world of the film noir as O'Brien, the victim of a slow-acting poison, crashes around San Francisco and Los Angeles like a human pinball in a marathon hunt for his killers. *D.O.A.* was released in 1949, at a time when there was a rich crop of B thrillers, among them Don Siegel's *The Big Steal,* Joseph H. Lewis' *Gun Crazy* and Joseph Lerner's *C-Man.* For cinema audiences wilting under the bloated vacuities of David O. Selznick's *Duel in the Sun* or the flabby heroics of Tyrone Power vehicles like *Captain of Castile,* the tight little thrillers of the late 40s and early 50s — hammered-down films noir or location-shot police procedure Bs — had the effect of a brief, jangling hop under a cold shower.

For postwar European cinemagoers they established a vivid, highly stylized picture of urban America. Just as Americans who had never visited Britain retained a notion of a fog-shrouded London straight out of *Hangover Square,* so their equivalents on the other side of the Atlantic daydreamed of the freeways, used car lots and seedy hotel lobbies of Los Angeles, and the men and women who populated them: double-crossing broad Rhonda Fleming in *Cry Danger;* trigger-happy hood Neville Brand in *D.O.A.* — 'he's an unfortunate boy, a psychopath', says Luther Adler regretfully as Brand readies himself to pistol whip the hapless Edmond O'Brien; cops with the Mob breathing down their necks, like Gig Young in *City That Never Sleeps;* and laconic, shop-soiled heroes, sometimes ex-cons with a past they would rather forget or, like John Payne in *The Crooked Way,* with one they cannot even remember.

Far from being films noir, the B thrillers of the 30s were affairs of black and white. There was no room for ambivalence as jut-jawed leading men Jack Holt, Don Terry and Brian Donlevy slugged their way through actioners like *Behind the Mask, Fight to the Finish* and *Burn Reckless.* After the success of *G-Men* in 1935, a cycle of low-budget imitations put stalwarts Richard Dix, Chester Morris, Preston Foster and Richard Arlen into big hats and trenchcoats and dourly on to the track of the racketeers. Titles like *Show Them No Mercy, Smashing the Rackets, Muss 'Em Up* and *Let 'Em Have It* guaranteed plenty of frantic action and grim retribution for the mobsters in the final reel. By the standards of the 30s the violence could be quite surprising; in *Show Them No Mercy,* swarthy hood Bruce Cabot has a neat row of holes machine-gunned into his shirt front by kidnap victim Rochelle Hudson.

The G-Men were tough characters. They could dish it out and take it in equal measure, even when the punishment was self-inflicted. In *Behind the Mask,* Jack Holt casually plugs himself in the arm in order to establish an alibi. Other conventions were rigidly observed. The G-Man often grows up in the same environment as his gangster enemies but has chosen the path of justice and virtue. If he is happily married, like Jack Carson in *Parole Fixer,* he will be shot in the back by a mobster before the end of the first reel. This tragedy is inevitably followed by a scene in which his widow bravely fights back the tears as the leading man breaks the grim news through gritted teeth, the slow mashing of the fedora in his hands the only sign of strong, repressed emotions.

Parole Fixer was one of many excellent Paramount B thrillers of the 30s. The studio could call on an impressive list of character actors — Lloyd Nolan, Anthony Quinn, J. Carrol Naish, Buster Crabbe, Akim Tamiroff — whose ability to alternate villainy and heroism with equal gusto ran through a number of high-quality Bs of the period — *King of Alcatraz, Hunted Men, Tip-off Girls, Illegal Traffic* and *Prison Farm.* In *Prison Farm,* directed by Louis King in 1938, J. Carrol Naish was superb as a brutal guard leaning on Lloyd Nolan, who played a heel with redeeming qualities with his customary assurance. Nolan was a good enough actor to move easily between both sides of the law, playing a G-Man in the 1937 *Undercover Doctor* and a sympathetic racketeer in *Hunted Men* in the following year.

With their reputation for tough, pacey and topical crime thrillers Warners were always quick to exploit a lurid newspaper headline. *Blackwell's Island* (1939) was based on real-life exposé of graft in a state prison and featured the young John Garfield as the reporter who blows the whistle on a corrupt governor. These B newsmen were a hardy breed, their professional lives resembling the famous description of the battle of Waterloo, 'one damn thing after another'. In Richard Fleischer's *Follow Me Quietly* (1949) a newspaper editor is tossed from his office window by a psychopath. The dying hack dictates the story of this own murder for the front page before expiring dramatically on the pavement. This would have hardly raised an eyebrow in RKO's 1939 *Twelve Crowded Hours* with Richard Dix and Lucille Ball, or *Time Out For Murder,* a 1938 Roving Reporters adventure directed by H. Bruce Humberstone with Michael Whalen and Chick Chandler. If the newshounds weren't getting fingered by racketeers in D. Ross Lederman's *I Was Framed* (1944), they were investigating the death of a friend and discovering that he had been murdered by the newspaper's editor, *Silent Partner* (1945). Female news cameramen, like Nancy Kelly in *Double Exposure* (1944), were apt to become the unwitting photographers of murder. Trouble lay in store for Douglas Kennedy when he attempted to expose the horrors lurking behind the walls of a state penitentiary in a Sam Katzman quickie for Columbia, *Chain Gang* (1950), directed by Lew Landers.

At the end of the 1930s Warners were still squeezing mileage out of the rackets in an enjoyable series of B thrillers with a aerial background starring Ronald Reagan. In *Secret Service of the Air, Code of the Secret Service, Smashing the Money Ring* and *Murder in the Air,* Reagan dealt with counterfeiters, alien smugglers and assorted villains, usually with a strong right hook. Fast-moving, uncomplicated, with a clean-limbed hero and occasional pauses for comic relief from Eddie Foy Jnr, these unpretentious little films reflected the straightforward elements which bound together the B thrillers of the 30s. Genteel private detectives in the Thin Man mould, like Reginald Denny and Gail Patrick in Robert Florey's *Preview Murder Mystery* (1936) and trench-coated G-Men like Richard

right
A preoccupied Robert Preston and Gail Patrick with a prone Lloyd Nolan in Robert Florey's 1938 *King of Alcatraz*. This magnificently crafted Paramount B boasted a remarkable cast list, including J. Carrol Naish, Harry Carey, Dennis Morgan, Richard Denning, Tom Tyler and Gustav von Seyfertitz.

below
After undergoing plastic surgery, hood Bruce Cabot is horrified to find his initials carved on his face in *Let 'Em Have It* (1935).

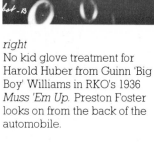

right
No kid glove treatment for Harold Huber from Guinn 'Big Boy' Williams in RKO's 1936 *Muss 'Em Up*. Preston Foster looks on from the back of the automobile.

left
Susan Hayward and Albert
Dekker in Stuart Heisler's 1941
Among the Living.

below left
Ronald Reagan and partner
enjoying the old-fashioned
methods of law enforcement in
Warners' *Secret Service of the
Air* (1939).

below
Peter Lorre and Evelyn Keyes
in Robert Florey's *The Face
Behind the Mask* (1941). Lorre
played a mobster whose
disfigured face was concealed
behind a contoured rubber
mask. The film's expressive
camerawork was by Franz P.
Planer.

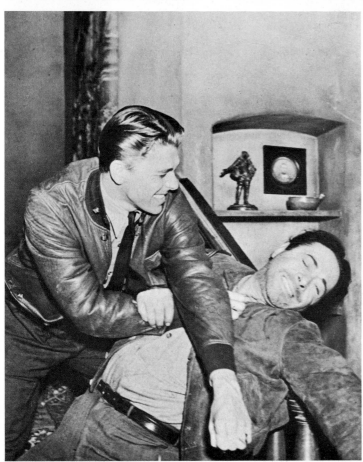

One of us will have to change. Erich von Stroheim and Dan Duryea in Anthony Mann's *The Great Flamarion* (1946). Infatuated vaudeville sharpshooter von Stroheim has killed Mary Beth Hughes' husband but is unaware that she is planning to run off with Duryea, the arch-cad of the 40s.

Butler Stanley Ridges has slipped some knockout drops into Edward Arnold's nightcap and is waiting for him to drink it but the blind sleuth is not so easily fooled. *Eyes in the Night* (1942), Fred Zinnemann's second (and last) B film for MGM, was an intriguing detective story in which Arnold played a blind private detective.

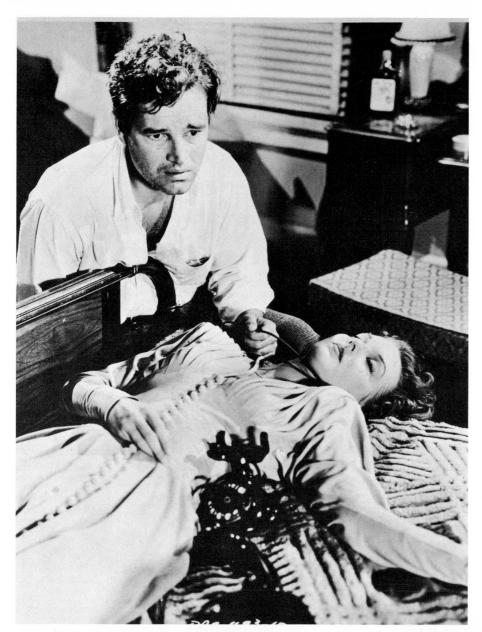

left
Tom Neal has accidentally
strangled Ann Savage in Edgar
Ulmer's B masterpiece *Detour*
(1946), shot in five days for a
mere $20,000.

below left
Nina Foch in Jospeh H. Lewis'
My Name Is Julia Ross (1945), a
little gem with fine supporting
performances from Dame May
Whitty and George Macready
as her psychopathic son. The
unsuspecting Foch is a pawn in
a plot to cover up the murder of
Macready's wife. The critic
James Agee wrote in *The Nation*
that the film was a 'successful
attempt to turn good trash into
decently artful entertainment',
though he was less happy with
Lewis' 'boom-happy' direction.

below right
Bad blood is thicker than water.
Claire Trevor and Lawrence
Tierney make an unlovely
couple in Robert Wise's *Born to
Kill* (1947).

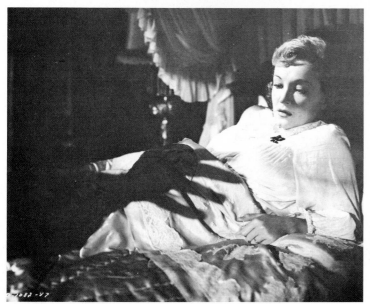

33

Arlen in *Let 'Em Have It* (1935) went about their work in a world where good and evil were sharply distinguished and malefactors were brought to book by the forces of law and order or their own megalomania. It would be an overstatement to say that in the following decade studios ceased to produce similar films. There was always a market for brisk little actioners like Universal's 1941 *San Francisco Docks.* Directed by Arthur Lubin and starring Burgess Meredith, Irene Hervey, Barry Fitzgerald and Robert Armstrong, it crammed both action and humour into its brief running time of 60 minutes. This allowed little time for sophisticated plotting and characterization, and in true B fashion we learn all we need to know about the two principals, Meredith and Hervey, in a 60-second argument at the beginning of the film. Playing a low-budget version of the Pat O'Brien two-fisted priest, Robert Armstrong brings matters to a conclusion by flooring the villain (Edward Pawley) in an alley.

Very much the formula B, *San Francisco Docks* took its place alongside a growing number of films which moved in a more complex ambiguous world, that of the film noir. Perhaps much of the charm of the film noir is that it exists in the eye of the beholder. Nevertheless, a number of elements can be isolated from the mass of films of the 40s and 50s which restrospectively have been placed in this category. Hollywood's discovery of psychoanalysis enabled writers and directors to produce psychological thrillers which gave their protagonists more complicated and ambivalent motivations. One of the first films to explore this murky area was Charles Vidor's 1939 *Blind Alley* with Chester Morris as an insane killer who holds psychiatrist Ralph Bellamy prisoner and then allows himself to be analyzed. Stuart Heisler's *Among the Living* (1941) and Boris Ingster's *Stranger on the Third Floor* (1940), also provided interesting signposts towards such later B classics of the genre as *The Locket,* and *Lady of Deceit.*

In *Among the Living,* Albert Dekker plays a dual role, a respectable businessman and his insane twin. Dekker's worse half escapes from the asylum, finding refuge in a seedy boarding house run by Maude Eburne and her sassy daughter, the young Susan Hayward. Soon he begins to kill, in a chilling touch pressing his victim's hands over her ears in a compulsive reminder of a youthful trauma — his mother's screams as she was beaten by his father. At the film's climax he is cornered in an abandoned house by the local townsfolk and subjected to trial by a kangaroo court reminiscent of that in Fritz Lang's *M.*

In *Stranger on the Third Floor,* Peter Lorre plays a faint B echo of that tortured soul, but the film's emphasis is on the confused mental state and vulnerability of its central figure, a journalist (John McGuire) whose testimony has sent an innocent man (Elisha Cook Jnr) to the death cell for the brutal murder of a local restaurant owner. McGuire's rising sense of guilt — and the sudden realization that his nasty little next door neighbour (Charles Halton) may well be the murderer's next victim — plunges him into a remarkable expressionist dream sequence. Its cross-hatched shadows and sharp, tilted camera angles, reminiscent of *The Cabinet of Dr Caligari,* are expertly captured by cameraman Nicholas Musuraca. (The tilted camera was also used to great effect by Edgar Ulmer in the flashback confession sequence in *Bluebeard.*) Halton's murder brings McGuire under suspicion and it is left to his girlfriend (Margaret Tallichet) to hunt down the real killer. The pursuit of a killer through a seedy or corrupt urban environment by a lone (and often innocent) woman is another recurring motif of Bs of the period, attaining its most satisfying realization in Mark Robson's *The Seventh Victim* (1943). In *Stranger on the Third Floor* the murderer is revealed as an escaped lunatic, the victim of harrowing experiments in a mental hospital. With great skill, in what is little more than a thumbnail sketch, Peter Lorre is able to elicit the audience's sympathy,

A cup of tea is called for as Edmond O'Brien gets a helping hand from Godfather Luther Adler after being pistol-whipped by the thuggish Neville Brand in Rudolph Maté's *D.O.A.* (1949). Maté had worked with Dreyer as cameraman on *La Passion de Jeanne d'Arc* (1928) and *Vampyr* (1932).

William Lundigan and Paul Bryer find the latest in a trail of corpses left by a mad killer, 'The Judge', in Richard Fleischer's *Follow Me Quietly* (1949). The killer only strikes at night and when it's raining, as is attested by the state of Lundigan's trench coat.

dying under the wheels of a truck and with his last breath telling the police, 'I'm not going back'.

Stranger on the Third Floor possesses most of the standard ingredients of the film noir. An urban setting in the seedy no-man's-land of frowsty boarding houses and cheap diners, a grease-stained universe whose squalor was exquisitely observed by Raymond Chandler's Philip Marlowe. A heavy dose of reach-me-down Freud, a compromised hero and a mentally disturbed killer are all seen through an expressionist glass darkly. Admittedly the low camera angles, perpetual night and menacing shadows of the film noir owe a debt to the Weimar backgrounds of such emigré directors as Edgar Ulmer, Rudolph Maté, Robert Siodmak and Otto Preminger; but there were other influences at work. The accumulating unease of the 40s, and the uncertainties of the postwar world, with its own menacing shadows of the Cold War and an imaginary Red menace at home, reinforced the bleak outlook of the film noir. The rash of postwar films in which amnesiac war veterans return home to stumble on the traumas of their forgotten lives reflect an unconscious desire to ignore the past and an unwillingness to face the future.

There were also more prosaic influences at play. The wartime constraints on building material led to the multiple use of cheaply constructed sets which were ideally shot in low-key light. This was made easier by the development of more sensitive, finely grained film stock, high-speed lenses and portable power units, which provided greater opportunity for virtuoso camerawork. Finally — and this is by no means insignificant when one considers that some of the finest noir films were originally scheduled as bottom-of-the-bill fodder — there were limitations inherent in a budget of $70,000 or less. As Nick Grinde breezily put it in an imaginary scenario, 'When John finally gets into the chase at the end of the picture, does he search the affluent Union League Club, or a museum, or the zoo? You guessed it, cousin, the scene is shot in an alley with three cops and some dandy shadows.'

Dandy shadows or not, the inhabitants of the film noir pick their way warily through a hostile universe whose shifting surfaces reflect pessimism, doomed obsessions, corruption and betrayal. In the film noir, nothing is ever quite what it seems. In Richard Fleischer's 1949 *Follow Me Quietly*, detective William Lundigan is faced with an outbreak of baffling murders, committed by a self-styled 'Judge' whose killing of public figures seems to be triggered by the onset of heavy rain. Not the brightest of cops, Lundigan is soon reduced to muttering about 'creeps, psychos and guys who read too many magazines'. In despair he constructs a faceless, suited and behatted dummy from the fragmentary clues left behind by the killer. In a police line-up this eerie, unconscious evocation of Magritte's dream world is propped up next to flesh-and-blood suspects. Lundigan keeps the dummy in his office, and late at night, in the darkened room, he taunts the inert, lumpish shape slumped in front of a rain-slashed window. As he leaves, the 'dummy' slides into life as the omnipresent 'Judge' makes good his escape.

The irrational forces at work in the film noir often erupt without warning into the humdrum lives of the principals. In *D.O.A.* Edmond O'Brien is a small-town accountant whose innocent involvement in a massive fraud leads to a slow, agonizing death. The paranoia with which the film is drenched lends a nightmarish quality to quite ordinary events. A salesmen's conference in O'Brien's hotel develops a shrieking intensity as portly executives cavort in the corridors in an unlikely and premonitory dance of death.

O'Brien's fate is determined from the first moments of the film. All he can do is search for the reasons in his past. Similarly, there is to be no reprieve for Tom Neal at the end of Edgar Ulmer's *Detour*. Neal plays a musician down on his luck hitchhiking to Los Angeles to see his girlfriend. He is given a lift by a rich, pill-popping wastrel (Edward Macdonald) who boastfully shows him the scars he has recently received at the hands of a stroppy female hitchhiker. After popping one pill too many Macdonald hits his head on a rock and pegs out. Neal takes his car, his clothes, his identity and in so doing signs away his own life. When he in turn stops to pick up a hitchhiker, the lift is the strident tubercular Vera (Ann Savage), the woman responsible for Macdonald's scars. Neal thinks his nightmare is over, but when she wakes from an exhausted sleep her first question is 'What did you do with the body?' Convinced that Neal must have murdered Macdonald, she eagerly blackmails him into selling the car. Then a newspaper report of the imminent death of Macdonald's millionaire father gives her a better idea. He has not seen his son since the latter's childhood, and she suggests that Neal impersonates him to collect the legacy — if he does not go along with her, she will telephone the police. In a drunken squabble Neal accidentally strangles her with a telephone cord. We leave him on the road, in limbo, condemned to wander the dingy backwaters of America in the certain knowledge that 'some day a car will pick me up that I never thumbed'.

Detour's minimal budget ($20,000), its harsh monotonal acting and sleazy 'poverty row' sets — Los Angeles is merely a back-projected car lot — provide Ulmer with the appropriate raw material to construct the chaotic, disordered world in which his characters move. Like the puppets in *Bluebeard's* Faust sequence, they are marionettes, jerked into life by forces beyond their control and existing 'only to suffer passively what happened to them'. In *Detour,* the feeling of helplessness is accentuated by the use of a narrative device which became the hallmark of the B film noir, the flashback accompanied by a numbed voice-over, which probes into the débris of the past, searching for the crucial moment, drawing the audience into the role of collective confessor.

In John Brahm's 1949 *The Locket,* the flashback technique is carried to extraordinary lengths, the film resembling a seemingly endless series of Chinese boxes as the audience strives to keep up with flashbacks within flashbacks within flashbacks. Laraine Day plays a plausible psychopath whose kleptomania is rooted in a childhood incident in which in humiliating circumstances she is forced by her housekeeper mother's employer to return a valuable locket given to her as a birthday gift by her employer's daughter. The trauma blights everything around her: an innocent man is condemned to death for a murder she has committed; an artist boyfriend (Robert Mitchum) is driven to suicide; and her husband (Brian Aherne) suffers a mental breakdown. The film opens with Aherne attempting to persuade her next victim on the morning of their wedding that his bride is a wrong'un and that he should cancel the ceremony. At the film's end he is brushed aside and, as Day prepares to walk down the aisle, the wheel swings full circle. For pressed into her hand is the locket — her future mother-in-law is the woman who deprived her of the fatal object in childhood and is now the unwitting agent of her destruction. Her slow progress towards the altar is like a Calvary, with the nightmares of the past crowding in on her, and she collapses, reduced to her former childish self.

The Locket is an extreme example of the streak of misogyny that runs through B thriller psychology. Lizabeth Scott killing everyone who gets in her way in Byron Haskin's 1949 *Too Late for Tears;* Claire Trevor, oozing contempt for everything in Robert Wise's *Born to Kill* (1947), her 'bad blood' impelling her into the murderous embrace of Laurence Tierney.

These greedy, powerful, deranged creatures often seem more vital than the genre's compromised leading men. Even when pursuing an active role

Dennis O'Keefe discovers a dead Mary Meade in Anthony Mann's *T-Men* (1947), whose shadow-drenched *mise-en-scène* undermines its semi-documentary trappings and plot – the break-up of a counterfeiting ring. Mann's assured noir style in *T-Men, Desperate* (1947) and *Raw Deal* (1948) owed much to an apprenticeship in Bs like *The Great Flamarion* and *Strange Impersonation* (1946).

There's an awful mess on the wall when Edmond O'Brien gets his man in Gordon Douglas' police procedure thriller *Between Midnight and Dawn* (1950).

John Carradine and Dean Jagger in Joseph Lerner's *C-Man* (1949), a stylish B made on a shoestring budget with an intriguing polytonal score by Gail Kubik.

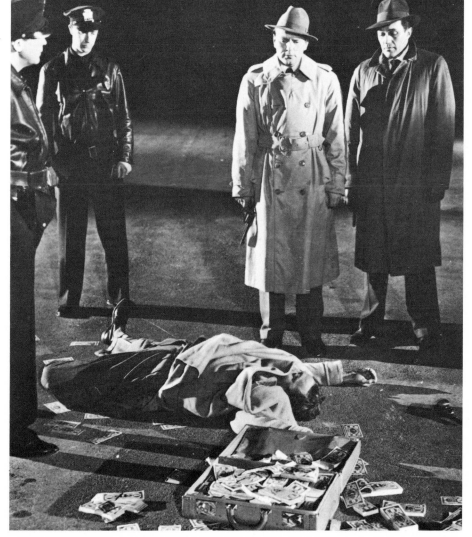

above
There are eight million fedoras in the naked city and here are two of them, Roy Roberts (left) and Scott Brady in Alfred Werker's *He Walked by Night,* a 1948 Eagle-Lion release. A year earlier Eagle-Lion, a distribution company owned by J. Arthur Rank, had absorbed PRC.

Nothing moves as Charles McGraw (centre) contemplates that crime does not pay in Richard Fleischer's *Armoured Car Robbery* (1950).

Mickey Rooney brawling with rival newsboy Douglas Croft at the start of Roy Rowland's boxing drama *Killer McCoy* (1947).

Dick Powell's impersonation of Philip Marlowe in Edward Dmytryk's *Murder My Sweet* (1944) gave him a new lease of life as a hard-boiled hero in a number of modest thrillers. Notable among them were Robert Parrish's *Cry Danger* (1950) and Anthony Mann's 1951 *Tall Target (left)* in which Powell played a discredited detective who thwarts Adolph Menjou's plans to assassinate Abraham Lincoln. In Robert Stevenson's 1948 *To the Ends of the Earth (bottom)*, he played a narcotics agent on the trail of a smuggling ring.

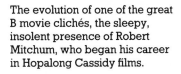

The evolution of one of the great B movie clichés, the sleepy, insolent presence of Robert Mitchum, who began his career in Hopalong Cassidy films.

top left
Ricardo Cortez, Mitchum and Laraine Day in *The Locket,* John Brahm's 1946 flashback extravaganza.

above
'The Devil got him first' – T-Man Gene Barry frisking moonshiner Mitchum in *Thunder Road* (1958), directed by the mysterious Arthur Ripley and based on an original idea by the star. One of the great 'road' movies.

top right
Mitchum at his most ironic in Jacques Tourneur's *Out of the Past* (1947), in which he provided the definitive numbed voice-over, hallmark of the film noir.

right
He looks in danger of falling asleep over Jane Greer in Don Siegel's *The Big Steal* (1949), an entertaining chase thriller with a neat twist at the end.

Blind love and funny walks. Peggy Cummins and John Dall in Joseph H. Lewis' existential masterpiece *Gun Crazy* (1949), riding a switchback of motiveless violence on their way to a savage end which prefigures *Bonnie and Clyde*.

Angst among the Festival of Britain bric-a-brac. Light years away from *Gun Crazy, The Techman Mystery* (1954), a genteel British thriller with John Justin and Margaret Leighton. The British never managed to imitate the thick ear stuff effortlessly accomplished by the Americans. However, they were on surer ground when attempting B versions of *Brief Encounter* with dead bodies in such programmers as the 'Edgar Wallace Mystery' films.

Racketeer Luther Adler gives testimony in Joseph Kane's *Hoodlum Empire* (1952).

The 'syndicate' was usually challenged by an individual motivated by revenge. Richard Kiley in Phil Karlson's *Phenix City Story* (1955), a raw account of the clean-up of 'Sin City', Alabama.

'First is first and second is nothing.' The new style of mobster, accountant Richard Conte, and the old style, Brian Donlevy, with deaf aid, in Joseph H. Lewis' *The Big Combo* (1955).

above
John Payne – on the floor – and Francis L. Sullivan in Phil Karlson's *Hell's Island* (1955), a freewheeling adaptation of *The Maltese Falcon* written by Karlson and Payne over a bottle of whisky.

below
Ralph Meeker (centre) as Mike Hammer, self-appointed scourge of the Reds in Robert Aldrich's *Kiss Me Deadly* (1955). Other Mike Hammers were Biff Elliot *I, the Jury* (1953), Robert Bray (*My Gun Is Quick, 1957*) and Micky Spillane himself in *Girl Hunters* (1963).

above
William Castle's comedy-thriller *Let's Kill Uncle* (1966) with Nigel Greene as a war hero who cheerfully tells his young nephew that he is going to kill him and make off with his inheritance. As the nephew is equally amoral, a hilarious contest ensues. The result is an honourable draw.

left
A homage to Warners' past. Ray Danton in Budd Boetticher's *The Rise and Fall of Legs Diamond* (1960).

below
Ann Jeffreys, Ludwig Stossel, Elisha Cook Jnr and Lawrence Tierney in Max Nosseck's *Dillinger* (1945).

they are fatally flawed. In *City That Never Sleeps,* Gig Young is a cop sliding into the pocket of Edward Arnold, an apparently successful businessman who is in fact only 60 per cent legitimate. His marriage is on the rocks (his wife has the gall to earn more than him) and he wants to run away with a hard-faced stripper played by that queen of floozies, Marie Windsor. (She has an extraordinary bump 'n' grind routine, seemingly coming off the stage with more costume than when she started.) In Joseph H. Lewis' *So Dark the Night* (1946) Steven Geray is a holidaying Parisian detective called in to investigate a double murder which by degrees he realizes has been committed by his own schizophrenic *alter ego.* In Lewis' *The Big Combo* (1955) Cornel Wilde's obessional pursuit of mobster Richard Conte is fuelled by a pathetic infatuation with Conte's classy moll, Jean Wallace.

Joseph H. Lewis' career provides a fine example of the highly crafted films that can be fashioned from the most unpromising material and in the most difficult conditions. With the exception of the costumer *The Swordsman* (1948) and the musical sequences from *The Al Jolson Story* (1947), Lewis devoted his considerable talents to making second features, the last, the 1958 *Terror in a Texas Town,* a bizarre Western shot on a minimal budget. The 1972 *International Encyclopedia of Film* does not give Lewis an entry, but in 1980 the Edinburgh Film Festival honoured him with a major retrospective which screened a wide selection of his work and not merely those films on which his reputation rests — *My Name Is Julia Ross, So Dark the Night* and *Gun Crazy.*

Lewis' movies — even journeyman efforts like *Blazing Six Shooters* (1941) — are distinguished by fluid camerawork. Intractable rubbish like *Secrets of a Co-ed* (1942) is temporarily brought to life with a court-room scene encompassed in a virtuoso ten-minute crane shot, a small miracle on a six-day shooting schedule. In his best work economic and elegant camera movements reflect and balance different characters' points of view while saving pages of dialogue, a vital skill when dealing with cramped running times of barely over an hour. In *So Dark the Night,* Steven Geray arrives at a country hotel in a chauffeur-driven car. In an eloquent and crisply edited silent sequence he is observed by the innkeeper's daughter (Micheline Cheirel). Her excited gaze slides across the gleaming coachwork and chrome fittings, leaving the audience in no doubt as to her character and her intentions. The long, tracking shot at the beginning of *Lady Without a Passport* is matched in brilliance by the famous single-take bank robbery in *Gun Crazy.* The camera placed in the back seat of the car turns the audience into an unnoticed eavesdropper as John Dall and Peggy Cummins swop tense, fractured remarks on their way to the hold-up. In *The Big Combo* Richard Conte twitches out aging hood Brian Donlevy's deaf aid before ordering his execution. We see the killing from Donlevy's point of view, the Thompson guns chattering away at us soundlessly.

From the moment Jean Wallace flees from her minders down a dark alleyway, we know that *The Big Combo* is located squarely in noir territory. Nevertheless by 1955, the year of its release, the classically organized noir film of the 40s, with its dark lighting and frequently over-upholstered psychology, was a museum piece. Even in *The Big Combo,* Jean Wallace's passivity at the hands of both Conte and Wilde is typical of the limp heroines of the 50s, light years away from voracious *femmes fatales* of the 40s, like Hedy Lamarr in Ulmer's *The Strange Woman* (1946).

In the late 40s the success of Jules Dassin's *Naked City* (1948), a location-shot police procedure film, led to a rash of B imitations tricked out with a hectoring March of Time commentary and moving out of the shadow-filled studio into the harsh, neon-lit streets of America's cities: *Motor Patrol,* directed by the prolific Sam Newfield, Gordon Douglas' *Between Midnight and Dawn,* and Alfred Werker's *He Walked by Night* provide good examples. There was an occasional interesting variation, as in *Trouble Preferred,* a female version in which two trainee women cops in Los Angeles are given the chance to unravel an attempted suicide. Solid little Bs like Frederick de Cordova's 1949 *Illegal Entry,* with Howard Duff and George Brent, adopted a semi-documentary approach to the smuggling of aliens. This racket had been a B standby since the 30s; Allan Dwan's 1936 *Human Cargo,* starring Brian Donlevy and Claire Trevor, provides a good example of the breed.

Alongside the sagas of prowl cars and motorcycle cops ran a series of films which concentrated on the forensic fight against crime. In John Sturges' *Mystery Street* (1950), the Harvard University Department of Legal Medicine uses the latest methods to reconstruct a murder and then finds the guilty man, among no fewer than 86 suspects, by scientific treatment of the victim's skeleton. In the same year Richard Fleischer's *Trapped,* starring Lloyd Bridges, pitted the US Treasury's boffins against a gang of counterfeiters.

These films are located in a confident world full of booming voice-overs cataloguing the invincible batteries of technology at the disposal of the forces of law and order, and montages of stern police officers rasping into desk microphones and moving little pins around on street maps. The villains are thus pinpointed and then hunted down. However, a cluster of movies from the early and mid-50s took a different line, seeking to expose the widespread corruption of American politics and big business which was eating away at the fabric of society. The enemy was no longer a lonely psychotic or a bunch of trigger-happy Paramount hoodlums led by a pop-eyed Akim Tamiroff. It was the 'syndicate', an octopus of graft and corruption whose tentacles spread into every corner of American life in the guise of 'legitimate' business. The films drew their often considerable raw vigour from the revelations of the Kefauver Committee, or to give it its full name, The Senate Special Committee to Investigate Crime in Interstate Commerce. To American cinemagoers Luther Adler's syndicate racketeer, testifying before a Senate committee in Joseph Kane's *Hoodlum Empire* (1952), seemed as real a bogeyman as the fellow travellers hauled in front of another committee unmentionable in Hollywood. Many of these exposés — *The Big Operator, Inside Detroit* (both dealing with union corruption) and Edward L. Cahn's *Inside the Mafia* — were somewhat less than searing. Nevertheless, in the hands of capable craftsmen like Byron Haskin and Phil Karlson, both adept at handling violent, blunt action, a number of films provided mirrors of the times.

Phil Karlson's *Phenix City Story* (1955) was based on the real-life clean-up of 'Sin City', Alabama, after the murder of a reforming attorney-general elect. Byron Haskin's *The Boss* (1956), with a fine performance as an underworld king by that underrated actor John Payne, took as its inspiration the downfall of the notorious Pendergast regime in Kansas City. Ironically, while these films advance an all-pervading underworld conspiracy, it is always run to ground and smashed by a crusading individual motivated by revenge (a theme which Karlson, in a long career, has taken up again and again). Moreover, the audience is left in no doubt that vice barons like Edward Anderson in *Phenix City Story* are merely the instruments of more powerful faceless men far removed from the bordellos and one-armed bandits of 'Sin City's' sleazy 14th Street. Far from being reassuring celebrations of American democracy and basic decency, they leave a worrying question mark hanging over the apparently unruffled surface of Eisenhower's America.

As the semi-documentary cycle sputtered to a halt, the gangster movie made a comeback in the form of biopics of celebrated hoodlums of the

Prohibition era — *Baby Face Nelson* (1957), *Machine Gun Kelly* (1958) and *The Rise and Fall of Legs Diamond* (1960).

For entirely understandable reasons the gangster movies of the early 30s avoided portrayals of recognizable crime Tsars, and after the success of *G-Men* in 1935 the emphasis was switched from the mobsters to law enforcement officers. In the following decade, during which the major studios prudently paid protection money to the syndicate and mobsters like Bugsy Siegel blackmailed big stars and their agents, there was a decided reluctance to revive the genre. It was left to 'poverty row' outfits like PRC and Monogram to make *Machine Gun Mama*, *Roger Touhy, Gangster* and *Dillinger*, and even these films dealt with the exploits of small gangs like Ma Barker's rather than the big time racketeers. Max Nosseck's *Dillinger* (1945), with Laurence Tierney, Anne Jeffreys and Elisha Cook Jnr, represented an effort by Monogram to move up-market. It was their first film released on a percentage, costing $193,000 (a huge outlay for Monogram) and grossing over four million dollars worldwide. Nevertheless, the films parsimonious producers, the King Brothers, still managed to incorporate into *Dillinger* sizeable chunks of action footage from Fritz Lang's 1937 *You Only Live Once*.

During the 50s the process of divestiture provided a vacuum which independents like AIP and Allied Artists filled with cheaply made original films, among them a cycle of gangster biopics initiated by Don Siegel's *Baby-Face Nelson* (1957), with Mickey Rooney as the eponymous hero. Roger Corman's 1958 *Machine Gun Kelly*, with Charles Bronson and Susan Cabot, is reminiscent of Ulmer's work at PRC. Its minimal production values and two-dimensional characters are contained in an amoral universe in which no attempt is made to locate them in an historical context or provide reasons for the random violence of the principals. Bronson and Cabot move

Adrift in an American limbo of seedy hotels and greasy diners – an Edward Hopper vision filtered through a B lens – Charles Bronson and Susan Cabot in Roger Corman's *Machine Gun Kelly* (1958).

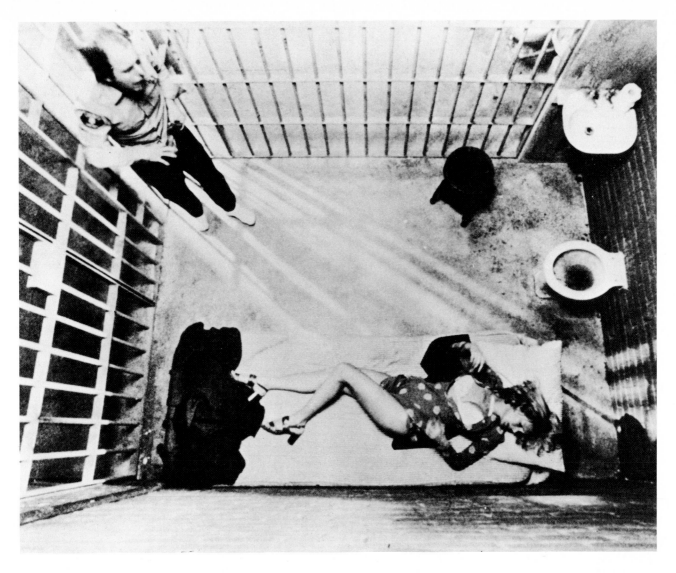

in a depopulated world of cheap hotels and crummy bars, the twilight zone through which John Dall and Peggy Cummins fled in *Gun Crazy* and in which Yvette Mimieux is stranded at the end of *Jackson County Jail* (1976). This makes a sharp contrast with the more traditional approach adopted by veteran action director William Witney in AIP's 1958 *The Bonnie Parker Story* and Budd Boetticher's *The Rise and Fall of Legs Diamond* (1960), released by Warners and a studied evocation of that studio's archaeology.

An interesting coda to these films was provided by two New World releases, *Big Bad Mama* (1974) and *The Lady in Red* (1979). In characteristic New World fashion they place a woman at the centre of events. In *Big Bad Mama,* which boasts a vibrant performance by Angie Dickinson, there is a straightforward attempt at role reversal with Dickinson playing Wilma McClatchie the leader of a gang of bank robbers consisting of her two daughters (Robbie Lee and Susan Sennett) and Tom Skerritt and William Shatner. Throughout the film Dickinson remains in charge. She plans the robberies and choses and rejects her lovers, assuming the traditional male role with her lover Tom Skerritt as she enters and undresses while he waits passively in bed. *The Lady in Red* combines the old AIP gangster biopic approach with the New World 'woman in jeopardy' angle, as Pamela Sue Martin suffers every kind of indignity on her way to becoming a fully-fledged gangster and a tiny footnote to history as John Dillinger's companion on the night the G-Men finally caught up with him.

Nightmare America comes looking for Yvette Mimieux in Michael Miller's *Jackson County Jail* (1976).

THE MULE COST NOTHING
SERIES
AND SERIALS

The series were one of the great staples of the Bs. They provided a proving ground for young actors and directors; ready work for studio contract players; and occasionally rest homes for stars past their peak. Frequently adapted from popular radio programmes or mass market fiction, their leading characters were instantly familiar to cinema audiences. And they were cheap. As director Arthur Lubin remarked of the 1949 *Francis*, the first in the Francis the Talking Mule series, 'Donald [O'Connor] got $30,000 at the time, the mule cost nothing'. Despite this, the mules (there were, in fact, three of them) continued to receive more fan mail than O'Connor or any of the contract starlets — Piper Laurie, Julia Adams, Martha Hyer — who were worked into the series by Univeral.

Arthur Lubin directed the first six films in the series, and then went on to create *Mr Ed,* a television series about a talking horse. The link with the small screen is apposite, as the television series now occupies the territory once held by its B equivalents of the 30s and 40s: private eye sagas, courtroom and hospital dramas, Westerns (dealt with in another chapter), domestic comedies and exotic adventures on a discernibly low budget. Indeed, from the early 50s many of the heroes of the Bs — Hopalong Cassidy, Tarzan, Dr Kildare, The Saint, Charlie Chan and Ellery Queen — found a new and lucrative home in television.

If the 40s were the era of the cynical private eye, straight from the pages of the hard-boiled school of Raymond Chandler, then the 30s were the heyday of the gentleman detective, a suave dilletante always several jumps ahead of the bumbling police on his way to an elegant unveiling of the villain in the final reel. The exemplar of the debonair amateur sleuth was Philo Vance, and his most accomplished screen impersonator William Powell, who played S. S. Van Dyne's character in four films, the first three for Paramount and the final one for Warners. Powell was followed by a number of disparate Vances in films which slid inexorably from programmer to B status. Basil Rathbone, Paul Lukas and Edmund Lowe all tried their hands in, respectively, *The Bishop Murder Case, The Casino Murder Case* and *The Garden Murder Case*. The results were none too happy — Rathbone was too stiff, Lukas too European and Lowe, with just a hint of a Brooklyn accent, was simply miscast.

Smooth Warren William played Vance in two films, *The Dragon Murder Case* (1934) for Warners and, after a gap of five years, Paramount's *The Gracie Allen Murder Case*. Principally a showcase for the klutzy Allen — at one point she calls William 'Fido Vance' — the film was nevertheless an

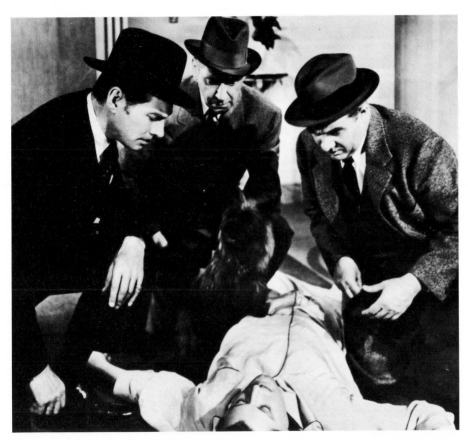

enjoyable mystery, with strong performances from Donald MacBride as District Attorney Markham and William Demarest as Sergeant Heath. In the following year Warners cast the British actor James Stephenson as Vance in *Calling Philo Vance*, a reworking of the William Powell classic *The Kennel Murder Case*, with the topical introduction of a spy plot. The urbane Stephenson, a rising star at Warners, died in 1941 and Philo Vance was not resurrected until after the war. In 1947, PRC's Howard Welsch did his best on that studio's minimal budgets, but his two Vances, William Wright in *Philo Vance Returns* and Alan Curtis in *Philo Vance's Gamble* and *Philo Vance's Secret Mission*, had none of the panache of William Powell's original.

James Stephenson (left) examines the inevitable corpse in Warners' *Calling Philo Vance* (1940), a stylish B remake of the *The Kennel Murder Case*, William Powell's farewell to the role of S. S. Van Dine's gentleman detective.

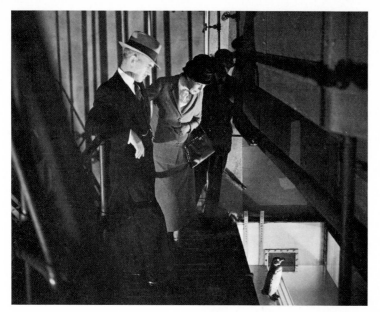

above
James Gleason, Edna May Oliver and Clarence H. Wilson attempt to reconstruct the events surrounding a bizarre murder in RKO's 1932 *The Penguin Pool Murder*, a Hildegarde Withers mystery.

above right
A two-faced Chester Morris in a rather unconvincing disguise in *Boston Blackie's Chinese Venture* (1949), the last entry in an entertaining Columbia series.

centre
Lloyd Nolan as private eye Michael Shane in *Dressed to Kill* (1941), one of a series of seven features for Fox. Henry Daniell is peering over his shoulder, Brett Halliday's Shane was a more realistic character than The Falcon or The Saint and in Nolan's capable hands spanned the gap between the heyday of the amateur sleuth and the hard-boiled gumshoes of the 40s.

right
A weary-looking Warner Baxter (left) ignores a diminutive gun as Dr Robert Ordway, a gangster turned criminal psychologist, in *Crime Doctor's Secret.* This Columbia series, which lasted until 1951, brought Baxter's career to a relatively dignified end after his nerous breakdown of the early 40s.

The decline of Philo Vance to the poverty row budgets of PRC highlights (albeit in exaggerated form) the fate that awaited all series. Once they were established, the initial eight-reel efforts gave way to six-reel supporting features. This was the lot of Warners' Perry Mason series which had been initiated in 1934 by *The Case of the Howling Dog* with Warren William giving Erle Stanley Gardener's attorney a svelte characterization far removed from Raymond Burr's performance in the long-running television series. However, after two years Warners pushed the series into the B category, bringing former silent star Ricardo Cortez into the Mason role in *The Case of the Black Cat* (1936) directed by journeyman William H. McGann, and wrapping up the series with a miscast Donald Woods in *The Case of the Stuttering Bishop* (1937).

Warren William was one of the B series' busiest leading men, in 1939 moving on from Philo Vance and Perry Mason to Louis Joseph Vance's gentleman thief Michael Lanyard, The Lone Wolf, a sophisticated ladies man who now operates on the right side of the law. The character had a long cinema history, going back to 1917 when Bert Lytell gave the first of his many performances as The Lone Wolf. In the sound era Melvyn Douglas and Francis Lederer both had a stab at the role, but Columbia found the perfect Lone Wolf in Warren William. He got off to a good start in 1939 with *The Lone Wolf's Spy Hunt;* Rita Hayworth played a Mata Hari-style spy and Ralph Morgan was her spymaster. Ida Lupino was the fetching heroine, an essential ingredient in all Lone Wolf adventures. Later films in the series — there were eight in the following years, the last *Passport to Suez* — were adorned by the comic presence of Eric Blore, Hollywood's most manic English butler. Three years after the Warren William series ended, Gerald Mohr, who usually played heavies, took over the role. The only remaining link with the past was the eye-rolling Blore and the series was abandoned after three films. There was another three-year gap before Ron Randell hammered the final nail into The Lone Wolf's coffin in *The Lone Wolf and His Lady.*

The Lone Wolf was not the only reformed criminal to delight cinema audiences of the 40s. Two successful series which used a similar device were the Boston Blackie adventures starring Chester Morris, and the Crime Doctor mysteries, which featured the dignified presence of the aging Warner Baxter.

Chester Morris was one of the most underrated leading men of the 30s and 40s, enlivening countless Bs with his spry wit and relaxed acting. This style was perfectly suited to the character of Boston Blackie, a former jewel thief operating as a freelance sleuth. Between 1941 and 1949 Morris made thirteen Boston Blackie Bs for Columbia, all of them whodunnits with a heavy leaning towards humour. The cracks in the frequently flimsy plots were papered over with the help of an excellent supporting cast — Richard Lane as Inspector Farraday, always struggling in Morris' wake, Blackie's sidekick the 'Runt' (George E. Stone), and Lloyd Corrigan, who played Arthur Manleder, a scatterbrained millionaire eager to do anything for a lark.

In the Crime Doctor series, based on Max Marcin's radio programmes, Warner Baxter played an amnesiac former gangster, Robert Ordway, who has become a leading criminal psychologist (a blow on the head reveals his past). There were ten films in the series, all of them bolstered with able supporting players like Ray Collins, Jerome Cowan, Steven Geray and John Litel. The sixth in the series, *Crime Doctor's Manhunt* (1946), directed by William Castle is of more than passing interest as Leigh Brackett's screenplay has a psychological theme which foreshadows Hitchcock's *Psycho* and Brian De Palma's *Sisters.* Ellen Drew plays a psychopath who assumes the physical appearance of her dead sister in order to kill. She almost succeeds in bumping off Warner Baxter before the police burst in to

right

The languid George Sanders in RKO's *The Saint in London* (1939) directed by John Paddy Carstairs and co-starring Sally Gray. Sanders played the Leslie Charteris character in four films before handing over the role to Hugh Sinclair.

below

George Sanders left The Saint series in 1942 to portray Michael Arlen's sleuth, The Falcon. He appeared in two Bs (*The Falcon Takes Over* and *The Falcon's Brother*) before his real-life brother Tom Conway assumed the part in nine more second features. Here he is, as quizzical and suave as Sanders, in *The Falcon in Hollywood* (1944). Co-star Veda Ann Borg is in the peaked cap. As a footnote, the first in the series, *The Falcon Takes Over,* was adapted from Raymond Chandler's *Farewell My Lovely.*

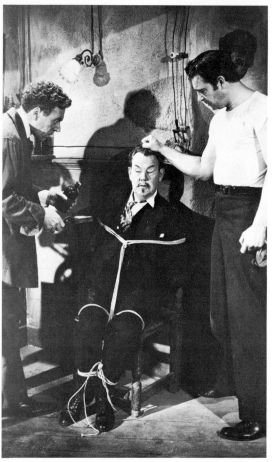

right

Lon Chaney Jnr has Sidney Toler in a painful grip as Leo G. Carroll contemplates something unpleasant with the sulphuric acid in *Charlie Chan in the City of Darkness,* directed by Herbert I. Leeds in 1939.

left
Harold Huber and Peter Lorre in *Mr Moto's Gamble* (1938).

below
A feeble attempt was made to revive the Moto series in 1965 with *The Return of Mr Moto*. Henry Silva played the Oriental sleuth, apparently unnoticed by the rest of the cast.

left
Bonita Granville as the precocious teenage sleuth Nancy Drew in *Nancy Drew, Troubleshooter* (1939).

carry her off. Baxter explains to dumb cop William Frawley that Drew is a schizophrenic. 'Say doctor', exclaims Frawley, 'I'd like to have you see my wife'. 'Split personality?' Baxter enquires. 'No personality', is the emphatic reply, reminding the audience that *Crime Doctor's Manhunt* is, after all, a B.

The series had their share of female sleuths, including the unlikely Hildegarde Withers, an overbearing middle-aged schoolmarm played by Edna May Oliver in three RKO Bs of the 30s, *The Penguin Pool Murder, Murder on the Blackboard* and *Murder on a Honeymoon.* Helen Broderick took over the role in *Murder on a Bridle Path,* and the series was wound up with two breathless performances by comedienne ZaSu Pitts in the *The Plot Thickens* and *Forty Naughty Girls.*

Aimed at a younger audience were four crisp little Warner Bs starring Bonita Granville as Nancy Drew, the teenage sleuth created by Carolyn Keene. Showing remarkable poise for one so young, she set about solving the mysteries into which her lawyer father (John Litel) had been drawn. The series was directed by a capable series hand, William Clemens. Clemens directed features in the Perry Mason, Dead End Kids, Philo Vance and Torchy Blane series. In the last the leading character was a frisky young girl reporter, initially played by Glenda Farrell. Barton Maclane was her boyfriend, Lieutenant Steve MacBride, modulating his voice only slightly from the constant bellow he employed in his gangster roles. Torchy's brains always got to the bottom of the mystery, but it usually required the combined brawn of Maclane and Sergeant Tom Kennedy to round up the villains. Jane Wyman played Torchy in the final film in the series, *Torchy Plays with Dynamite,* and Allan Jenkins took over the Barton Maclane role.

A role similar to that of Lieutenant MacBride was played by Grant Withers in Monogram's Mr Wong series. As Captain Street, a specialist in the thick ear school of detection, he was required to effect final-reel rescues of Boris Karloff's courteous, scholarly Oriental detective. Peter Lorre's Mr Moto provided more athletic performances in a series of eight films produced by Warners between 1937 and 1939. With good supporting casts — the two chief suspects in *Mr Moto Takes a Vacation* were Lionel Atwill and Joseph Schildkraut — and a lively Moto from Lorre, the series was a success. Nevertheless, it came to an end in 1939 at a time when Lorre was commanding larger roles and the situation in the Pacific ruled out a Japanese hero.

Mr Moto's occasional excursions into ju-jitsu contrasted sharply with the sedentary methods of the most popular of all Oriental detectives, Charlie Chan. Between 1931 and 1942 Fox produced 27 Chan adventures, the first sixteen featuring the Swedish actor Warner Oland. When Oland died in 1937, Sidney Toler took over the role and with it Chan's inimitable stock of sub-Confucian aphorisms: 'Bad alibi like dead fish — cannot stand test of time', or 'Insignificant molehill sometimes more important than conspicuous mountain'. In 1944 the series moved to Monogram, where a combination of poverty-row budgets and Toler's increasingly obvious lack of interest led to a sharp decline in quality. Toler died in 1947 and the series staggered to an end with Roland Winters in the Chan role in six films, the last of which, *Sky Dragon,* was released in 1949. Despite the efforts of veteran directors Derwin Abrahams, Lesley Selander and William Beaudine, and the appearance of such seasoned players as Evelyn Brent, Robert Livingston and Lyle Talbot, the series declined during this period from the bad to the virtually unwatchable.

The development of a Charlie Chan feature always led to the gathering of the suspects in a room and the unmasking of the guilty one by Chan, exclaiming in his fractured English, 'You are murderer!' This blunt dénouement invariably elicited an instant confession from the villain or, failing that, a desperate attempt to escape. Why the wretches never chose to brazen it out with the frequently bluffing Chinaman must remain one of the great mysteries of cinema. The 'instant confession' syndrome still afflicts assorted character actors thrust into this invidious position, and can be observed at work in the farfetched courtroom shennanigans of the TV series *Petrocelli*.

Sidney Toler and Warner Oland may have been as authentically Chinese as chop suey, but Basil Rathbone was every inch that great detective and representative of the more eccentric wing of the British upper middle classes, Sherlock Holmes. In two A features for Fox, *The Hound of the Baskervilles* and *The Adventures of Sherlock Holmes*, Rathbone gave perhaps the definitive screen performance as Holmes. Subsequently he played in a series of twelve Holmes adventures for Universal accompanied by his Fox partner, Nigel Bruce, as Doctor Watson. Much to the horror of the purists all of them were updated and in some, particularly *Sherlock Holmes and the Secret Weapon,* Rathbone sported a strange and singularly un-Holmesian haircut. The early adventures in the series were given wartime settings, complete with the Axis spy-secret formula plots which invaded all the genre Bs of the period. Unfailingly they concluded with a stirring address from Rathbone about the joys of democracy while Watson burbled away in the background. Four of the series had a distinct horror element — *The Scarlet Claw, The House of Fear, The Pearl of Death* and *The Spider Woman* — the last two launching Rondo Hatton and Gale Sondergaard respectively on independent B horror careers.

Another British stalwart who received the Hollywood treatment was Bulldog Drummond. 'Sapper's' character was the most popular of that clutch of granite-jawed clubland heroes of the 30s whose strong-arm methods, raging xenophobia and barely disguised anti-Semitism make their exploits less attractive reading today. Among several attempts to bring the novels to the screen was a Paramount series of seven adventures starring the American John Howard as Drummond, E. E. Clive as his devoted manservant and Reginald Denny as his dense pal Algy. In six of the films Heather Angel played Drummond's fiancée Phyllis Clavering — 'the swine! they've got Phyllis!' is never far from Drummond's lips as scheming foreigners abduct her in episode after episode.

In the first three films in the series the part of Drummond's foil, Inspector Nielson, was played by John Barrymore, clearly well past his prime, and after an initially lively performance in *Bulldog Drummond Comes Back,* clearly bored and somewhat the worse for drink. Barrymore was eventually replaced by the distinguished presence of H. B. Warner. The Drummond series was typical low-budget action fare, each feature running at a little over 60 minutes and with little effort made to create the Hollywood England whose anachronisms add a dreamlike charm to films like *Mrs Miniver.* They were principally held together by a number of splendid villains, including J. Carrol Naish, George Zucco and Eduardo Ciannelli. In *Arrest Bulldog Drummond,* Zucco is in vintage form. About to release a struggling netful of Drummond's colleagues into a particularly unpleasant pit of slime, he asks the smouldering hero, 'Care to come and see the splash'.

The British themselves provided some diverting series in the American mould. Sexton Blake, a comic strip echo of Sherlock Holmes, was played by George Curzon in three thrillers of the 30s. The 1938 *Sexton Blake and the Hooded Terror* was enlivened by a ripe performance as a master criminal by Tod Slaughter, one of British theatre's great hams. In 1944 David Farrar played Blake in *Meet Sexton Blake* and *The Echo Murders,* and Geoffrey Toone provided a 50s afterthought in *Murder on Site Three.*

right
A resolute Richard Dix
confronts J. Carrol Naish, the
man he has hired to kill him, in
William Castle's *The Whistler*
(1944), a memorable first entry
in a short Columbia series
which lasted from 1944 to 1947.

below
Harold Peary as The Great
Gildersleeve in *Gildersleeve on
Broadway*, directed in 1943 by
Gordon Douglas. The RKO
series was based on a character
from the Fibber McGee and
Molly radio show.

above right
Harassed Arthur Lake, lovely
young Rita Hayworth and Penny
Singleton as the eponymous
heroine of *Blondie on a Budget*
(1940) directed by Frank
Strayer.

right
Joe Kirkwood as the naive
young boxer Joe Palooka and
Leon Errol as Knobby Walsh,.
his wheeler-dealer promoter, in
Joe Palooka Champ (1946)
directed by Reginald LeBorg.
LeBorg directed five more
entries in this Monogram series
based on Ham Fisher's comic
strip.

above
Ann Sothern and Red Skelton in MGM's *Maisie Gets Her Man* (1942) directed by Roy Del Ruth. Maisie was a chorus girl forever finding herself stranded in unlikely situations. The first film in the series, *Congo Maisie* (1939) was a straight lift from *Red Dust*, with Sothern playing the Harlow role.

above
Ain't he cute? Micky Rooney as a flustered class president and Kathryn Grayson as his aide in MGM's *Andy Hardy's Private Secretary* (1941). Serial veteran George B. Seitz directed.

right
Jimmy Lydon strikes up the band in *Henry Aldrich For President* (Paramount, 1941) directed by Hugh Bennett.

below
Son of Rusty, second in a Columbia boy-and-dog series starring Ted Donaldson as the boy part of the duo. This 1947 B was directed by the ever dependable Lew Landers.

below
Lionel Barrymore, Lew Ayres and Lynn Carver in MGM's *Young Dr Kildare*, the first of a long series of hospital dramas. This one was directed by Harold S. Bucquet in 1938.

In 1948-49 Dick Barton, the hero of a popular British radio serial, was brought to the screen by Excelsior Films in three low-budgeters starring Don Stannard. Sadly the 15-minute radio thrills, which neatly evoked the American Dick Tracey serials of the 30s, produced howls of laughter when served up in feature form. Eventually the films were edited down to provide excitement for a more appropriate audience, the Saturday-morning children's show. Finally there were the Paul Temple films based on Francis Durbridge's radio sleuth. John Bentley as Temple and Dinah Sheridan as his wife provided a Home Counties version of Nick and Nora Charles in several second features of the late 40s, including *Calling Paul Temple* (1948) and *Paul Temple's Triumph* (1950).

While detective series were the most numerous of the genre, there were also many celebrations of domesticity and small-town life, the most successful of which were MGM's Andy Hardy films. The series was prompted by the 1937 *A Family Affair* in which Lionel Barrymore played teenager Mickey Rooney's father, Judge Hardy. In the first entry of the series proper, the part of the judge was played by Lewis Stone. Viewed today, the fifteen Hardy films made between 1937 and 1947 are drenched in an almost insufferable sentimentality. Andy Hardy's family (mother Fay Holden, sister Cecilia Parker, and Sara Haden as kindly Aunt Millie) are about as unreal as the the little town of Carver in which they live. In addition, Rooney's frantic mugging and camera hogging are particularly tedious. Directed with considerable ingenuity by serial veteran George B. Seitz, the films reflect the values of a Hollywood which has long since vanished. Their celebration of a fantasy America seems as silly as depictions of the English countryside in postwar British Bs like *Brandy for the Parson*. Nevertheless, Americans cling tightly to their fantasies. Thus it was not surprising to record that in 1942 the Andy Hardy series received an Academy Award for 'furthering the American way of life'.

Andy Hardy had an imitator of sorts in Henry Aldrich. The origins of the truly awful Henry Aldrich — the dumbest and most tiresome teenager of all time — lay in a stage play, *What a Life*, by Clifford Goldsmith. This was followed by a radio show and two relatively successful films with Jackie Cooper playing Aldrich. The screenplays were written by Charles Brackett and Billy Wilder. However, they were not involved in the subsequent series of nine Henry Aldrich films, which featured Jimmy Lydon as the eponymous moron and which ran from 1941 to 1944. John Litel played Henry Aldrich's father and Vaughan Glaser his long-suffering high school head, driven to understandable distraction in efforts like *Henry Plays Cupid*, in which his unruly pupil decides that he would be better off with a wife, in the form of Vera Vague. Every series had to have an episode revolving around a spooky, supposedly haunted house, and Henry Aldrich was no exception; in *Henry Haunts a House*, Jimmy Lydon plunges into a ghostly mix-up in an old dark house while searching for the missing Vaughan. Most of the Aldrich films were directed by Hugh Bennett.

Spooks, in the form of a weary looking Bela Lugosi, were trundled on in Monogram's *Spooks Run Wild*, an embarrassingly low-budget Bowery Boys adventure with Huntz Hall and Leo Gorcey. The Bowery Boys were the distant descendants of the 1937 Warner feature *Dead End*, starring Humphrey Bogart. Twenty years later, and approaching middle age, the weasel-faced Hall was still playing adolescents, having mugged his way through such low-budget variations on the Dead End theme as *The Little Tough Guys*, the *Junior G-Men* serial and The East Side Kids series.

Light years away from the urban problems of the Bowery Boys were the very suburban adventures of William Brown, the scruffy little schoolboy hero of Richmal Crompton's much-loved 'William' books. In 1948 they were brought to the screen in a British series which began with *Just William's Luck*. William Graham was the unkempt miniature anarchist, and Garry

Marsh and Jane Welsh his long-suffering parents. The best William books paint a marvellous picture of English middle-class life between the wars, full of ironic writing seemingly aimed at adults rather than children, but the films contained none of these subtleties.

As long-lived as Andy Hardy was the Blondie series, in its early years at least a satisfactory adaptation of Chic Young's comic strip featuring a scatterbrained housewife and her harassed, put-upon office worker husband Dagwood Bumstead. The first film in the series, *Blondie*, was released in 1938 and was directed by Frank Strayer, who handled many of the subsequent 28 films which spanned the next thirteen years. Arthur Lake played Dagwood, Penny Singleton was Blondie and Jonathan Hale was Mr Dithers, Dagwood's boss (the role was later taken over by that skilful character actor Jerome Cowan). Baby Dumpling was played by Larry Simms and, in a rare concession to reality, was allowed to grow up with the series, acquiring the name of Alexander in no. 11. There was also the scene-stealing dog, Daisie, and Irving Bacon as Mr Beasly, the hapless postman who is the regular victim of Dagwood's headlong dashes to the office. As with all long-running series, Blondie gave Columbia the opportunity to introduce young faces to a wider audience. Rita Hayworth appeared in *Blondie on a Budget;* Glenn Ford in *Blondie Plays Cupid,* and Larry Parks in *Blondie Goes to College.*

Medical dramas have a long history and are still popular today. In a big hospital all human life is conveniently contained. Jean Hersholt starred in a half-forgotten series as Dr Christian in the late 30s, but it was eclipsed by the immense success of MGM's Dr Kildare films, which ran from 1938 to 1947. The first in the series was *Young Dr Kildare* starring Lew Ayres as the idealistic young doctor and Lionel Barrymore as the irrascible Dr Gillespie. Set in the vast Blair General Hospital the cast of running characters — nurses, ambulance drivers, switchboard operators, even Kildare's benevolent parents — was longer than in the average series. Lionel Barrymore was the only character to see the series out. Lew Ayres left after *Dr Kildare's Victory* (1941), along with his parents Emma Dunn and Samuel S. Hinds. Laraine Day, Kildare's romantic interest, left in the same year, and Marilyn Maxwell moved in to bat her eyelids at Van Johnson. Dutch leading man Philip Dorn also had a stab at the Kildare role in *Calling Dr Gillespie*, and rugged James Craig was the final Kildare in *Dark Delusion.*

One step down from the series was the serial, the 20-minute cliffhanger which glued countless children to their Saturday-afternoon cinema seats from the silent era to the early 50s. Between 1929 and 1956, 231 serials were churned out by Hollywood, the great majority by Republic, Columbia and Universal. Frequently they were adapted from comic strips (*Spy Smasher, Flash Gordon, Batman, Superman, Dick Tracy, Terry and the Pirates*) or popular radio programmes and pulp fiction (*The Green Hornet, The Shadow, Captain Midnight, The Spider*). They provided a child's view of the universe, full of secret passwords, underground hideouts, snarling masked villains, evil jungle priestesses and chaotic, disordered violence. Their primitive, non-stop action and arbitrary suspension of the law as of cause and effect often give them a surreal quality amid the cheap sets, stock footage, and one-note acting. In Mascot's *Phantom Empire* (1935), an early Gene Autry vehicle, the cowboy star spends his time galloping between 'Radio Ranch' and a bizarre underground civilization, Murania, a kind of cut-rate version of *Things To Come,* located at the bottom of a disused mineshaft. In the final episode Murania is destroyed by a death ray. Autry rides back to the ranch to sing 'Silver-Haired Daddy of Mine'.

The most fondly remembered and frequently revived of the serials are the exploits of Flash Gordon, the hero of Alex Raymond's elegant comic

right
Buster Crabbe in a typical
chapter ending in Universal's
classic serial *Flash Gordon*
(1936).

below right
Tom Tyler does credit to his
tailor as Captain Marvel, all set
to do battle with the
megalomaniacal Scorpion in
Republic's 1941 serial
Adventures of Captain Marvel.

below
Gene Autry menaced with a
strange device after a wardrobe
raid in the lost city of Murania,
the setting of the 1935 Mascot
serial *Phantom Empire,* a
surreal blend of science fiction
and horse opera.

right
Bela Lugosi is not only upstaged by his own robot in Universal's 1939 serial *The Phantom Creeps*, but also appears to be having trouble with his digital watch.

below
Tony Barrett (centre) and Richard Powers (former cowboy star Tom Keene) see an opportunity to seize control of an underground racket when they discover their boss Jack Lambert apparently dying in RKO's *Mark of the Claw* (1947), a B feature based on Republic's four successful Dick Tracey serials which ran from 1937 to 1941. Ralph Byrd reassumed the role of the fearless detective, hero of Chester Gould's comic strip.

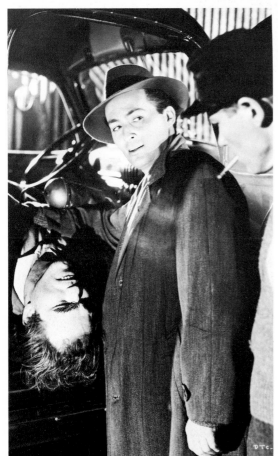

above
Villainy of a superior brand. Henry Brandon as Sax Rohmer's devil incarnate, Fu Manchu, in Republic's 1940 serial masterpiece *Drums of Fu Manchu*.

His vision evidently obscured, The Lightning (left) stands passively by as John Picciori gets Eleanor Stewart in his clutches in Republic's *Fighting Devil Dogs* (1938). Co-directors of this pulsating serial were action experts William Witney and John English.

Kane Richmond rests his chin on a right hook in *Spy Smasher* (Republic 1941).

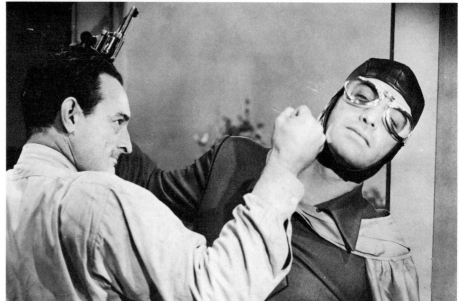

Charles Quigley turns the tables on one of the serials' greatest masked villains in Republic's *The Crimson Ghost* (1946). The heavy on the left is Clayton Moore.

left
What's going on? David Sharpe doubles for Tristram Coffin, the hero of Republic's *King of the Rocket Men* (1949).

centre
Is that a pistol in your pocket or are you just pleased to see me? Jut-jawed Jack Holt (left) faces down the heavies in Columbia's 1941 *Holt of the Secret Service*.

below left
Undaunted by the lack of a front on their car, Lloyd Bridges and Key Luke are on the track of Nazi agents in *Secret Agent X-9* (Universal, 1945), an updated version of an Alex Raymond comic strip. The first Secret Agent X-9 serial in 1937 starred Scott Kolk.

below right
Ken Howell, the clean-cut type in the centre, is droning on about the exploits of his G-Man brother in *Junior G-Men*, a 1940 Universal serial with the Dead End Kids. Huntz Hall (in baseball cap) looks distinctly unimpressed.

strip, which were first brought to the screen in 1936 by Universal. *Flash Gordon* starred Buster Crabbe, an Olympic swimming champion, sometime law student and bit-part actor — in 1933 he had taken the leading role in a ramshackle Principal Pictures serial, *Tarzan the Fearless*. Crabbe beat better-known actors like Jon Hall to the part, bleached his hair and secured a place among cinema's immortals.

Following the success of the first Raymond adaptation, Universal made two more Flash Gordon serials, *Flash Gordon's Trip to Mars* (1938) and *Flash Gordon Conquers the Universe* (1940). Jean Rogers played Dale Arden in the first two, and was replaced by Carol Hughes in the third. Their scientist companion, Dr Zarkov, was played by Frank Shannon and their deadly enemy, Ming the Merciless, tyrant of the planet Mongo, was Charles Middleton. While Ming lusted after the lovely Dale, his daughter, the curvaceous Princess Aura (Priscilla Lawson), cast longing glances at athletic, virile Flash. For 37 episodes Flash battled the power-crazed Ming, the latter hell-bent on Earth's destruction, using everything from a device to drain the atmosphere of nitrogen to seeding the air with a deadly dust called 'The Purple Death'. On their way to ridding the universe of Ming, Flash and the alternately swooning and shrieking Dale confronted Lion Men, Shark Men, giant Orangapoids, the Clay People and the Tree People, not to mention Azura, Queen of Magic (Beatrice Roberts), and cohorts of Ming's inept henchmen. Having survived death in the Tunnel of Terror and the Disintegrating Room in the first two serials, Ming was finally despatched in spectacular style at the end of the third by one of his own rocket warheads.

The Flash Gordon serials succeeded in creating the self-contained universe which is the basis of all sustained fantasy, although their frequently cardboard special effects and monsters necessarily strayed a long way from the crisp draughtsmanship of Alex Raymond's comic strip. Another great comic strip hero, Dick Tracey, had an easier passage from the page to the screen, principally because of the contemporary setting of the adventures and Ralph Byrd's splendid portrayal of the celebrated sleuth.

The essential ingredient in every serial chapter was the cliffhanging ending: we leave the hero lying unconscious in the path of an advancing tide of acid; chained to a stake while flames leap up around him; locked in a room while a strange gas freezes him to death; or trapped by an electrical death ray. Invariably he makes it, shaken but unharmed, into the next episode. His simple elimination was far too mundane a matter for the Machiavellian minds of super-criminals bent on world domination. A swift despatch was reserved for the villain's bumbling minions.

When they were well-drawn and played by experienced heavies, the serial villains were frequently far more interesting than the heroes who thwarted their mad schemes: music-loving George J. Lewis strumming 'The Moonlight Sonata' as he orders gangland executions in *Federal Operator 99* (Republic, 1945); Eduardo Ciannelli trying to control his lumbering sardine-can robot in *Mysterious Doctor Satan* (Republic, 1940); Lorna Gray radiating evil as Vultura in *Perils of Nyoka* (Republic, 1942); Carol Forman as the murderous Sombra in *The Black Widow* (Republic, 1947).

The evil representatives of the Yellow Peril infest the serials. As the Japanese Daka in Columbia's 1943 *Batman*, J. Carrol Naish instantly clambers over the top and keeps on going. More sinister was Henry Brandon as Sax Rohmer's perennial arch-fiend in Republic's 1940 *Drums of Fu Manchu*. Then there was a small army of masked masterminds, the possessors of assorted infernal devices, and all of them one simple aim, world domination. In *The Adventures of Captain Marvel* (Republic, 1941), the hooded Scorpion's atom-smashing device threatened freedom and democracy. *The Crimson Ghost* (Republic, 1946), hiding behind an alarming death's head, aims to turn the deadly cyclotrode on the helpless population. To further his ends he develops a 'control collar', which when placed around his victims' necks turns them into zombies, obeying his every instruction. In *Dick Tracey vs. Crime, Inc.* (Republic, 1941) The Ghost uses a weird machine to make himself invisible. The Lightning, the villain of the marvellously titled *Fighting Devil Dogs* (Republic, 1938) has a devastating electrical gun which he wields with deadly effect before being cornered by Lee Powell and Herman Brix.

In their heyday serials were shot in a month. Fifteen chapters were the classic length — of 57 Columbia serials only two, *Mandrake the Magician* (12) and *Brenda Starr, Reporter* (13), dipped below the magic number. (Republic favoured twelve chapters; 43 of their 66 serials fell into this format.) Two directors were customarily employed: one shot the dialogue scenes and fights, the other the outdoor action. In *Phantom Empire*, Otto Brower combined with one of Republic's many capable Western hands, B. Reeves Eason. For the follow-up, *Undersea Kingdom* with Ray 'Crash' Corrigan, Eason worked with Joseph Kane. By the early 50s, with the chill winds of television gusting through the serial units, the pace became even more frenzied. Spencer Gordon Bennet, a veteran of Republic Bs, was required by Columbia to shoot a series singlehanded in two weeks. The hard-working Bennet made twenty-one serials and, understandably, lavish use was made of stock footage from the studio's library. Republic's economical hand reached far back into the past: the 1952 *Zombies of the Stratosphere* had to make do with the twelve-year-old robot from *Mysterious Doctor Satan.*

For all-action fare it was difficult to beat Republic at its peak. Behind the camera was a team of capable directors — William Witney, John English, Eason, Brower — who could be relied upon to keep the pace fast and furious. In front of the camera, thrills and action were provided by brilliant stuntmen like David Sharpe, Tom Steele and Dale Van Sickel; Helen Thurston was a superb stuntwoman, doubling for Frances Gifford in *Jungle Girl* (1941). Serial stuntmen had a busy time, usually playing several thinly disguised roles as minor heavies as well as doubling for the hero in fights. In order to avoid drawing attention to their frequent reappearance at different stages in the plot, the camera hangs back from the action, providing the audience with the jumbled melées which filled the screen at regular intervals.

A particular advantage which Republic enjoyed over other studios was the splendid miniature department run by the Lydecker brothers. The Spider's Flying Wing from *Dick Tracy* was so successful that it was used again to convey The Lightning in *Fighting Devil Dogs*. One small but characteristic Lydecker effect was the spectacular destruction of a gas tank at the end of the first chapter in *The Masked Marvel* (1943).

As with B features, it was all too easy to become typecast as a serial hero. A few big names served an apprenticeship in the serials before escaping to bigger things. Ruth Roman made an early appearance in Universal's *Jungle Queen* (1945), Lloyd Bridges played Secret Agent X-9 in the same year. At the beginning of the 30s George Brent was upstaged by Rin Tin Tin in Mascot's *Lightning Warrior*. John Wayne made three serials for Mascot in this period, *The Shadow of the Eagle, The Hurricane Express* (both 1932) and *The Three Musketeers* (1933). Others were not so fortunate. Leading men like Kane Richmond, Kirk Alyn, Charles Quigley and Judd Holdren will be remembered, if at all, for their serial roles. Ralph Byrd became so identified with Dick Tracey that in later years he found it all but impossible to get work. The same fate overtook television's Superman George Reeves. After his suicide he was buried wearing his Superman cape.

Jungle Adventures

left
Herman Brix (later Bruce Bennett) and lethargic lion in the 1935 serial *New Adventures of Tarzan,* shot in extremely primitive conditions in Guatemala.

right
Clayton Moore (prodding) and Phylis Coates in what is generally regarded as Republic's most dismal serial, *Jungle Drums of Africa* (1953).

left
Johnny Sheffield on the studio backlot in *Bomba on Panther Island* (1949) directed by Ford Beebe and one of eleven Monogram Bs spun off from the Tarzan series in which Sheffield played Boy. The producer was Walter Mirisch, who went on to better things.

right
Frances Gifford tries to attact the attention of a passing gorilla in *Jungle Girl* (Republic, 1941).

BOOTS OF DESTINY
WESTERNS

An important landmark in the B Western's dusty road to death occurred in 1953, when the New York Theatre in Times Square ceased to show horse operas and began to book Italian art films. Built ten years before, as an East Coast equivalent of Hollywood's Hitching Post Theatre, the majority of its programmes had consisted of the 60-minute oaters which for two decades had formed the backbone of all-American action entertainment. Regular customers could expect double bills featuring their favourite sagebrush heroes: a Tim Holt adventure paired with Charles Starrett in his role of the Durango Kid; or a show featuring the two kings of the Singing Cowboys, Roy Rogers and Gene Autry. As the supply of B Westerns slowly dried up in the early 50s, and stars like Johnny Mack Brown, Allan Lane, Monte Hall and Lash La Rue faded from the screen, it became increasingly difficult for the theatre to maintain its programmes. Fittingly the New York Theatre's final Western show featured Gene Autry's farewell to Columbia, *The Last of the Pony Riders*, released in November 1953 and co-starring his old comic sidekick Smiley Burnette. By then Autry and his Flying A company were busy producing the first of the 85 30-minute television shows that were to become one of the staples of small screen entertainment.

By the end of the silent era, the Western had reached a low ebb. Stars like Jack Hoxie and the great Tom Mix had been quietly put out to grass and were rubbing along with tent shows and rodeo appearances. The first low-budget all-talking Western was the 1929 *Overland Bound* directed by and starring the portly Leo Maloney, a canny veteran of the silents. However, the pioneering film maker did not long survive his movie's release by Presidio onto the independent circuit and the favourable reviews it attracted in the trade press. During a protracted celebration at New York's Astor Hotel he succumbed to a heart attack.

The fortunes of the Western were not revived solely by the coming of sound, or by the singlehanded efforts of Leo Maloney. More important was the decision by Universal Studios to breathe life into a market which in the mid-20s had provided them with a major moneyspinner. Hedging their bets, they turned to the cowboy stars of the silents, Hoot Gibson and Ken Maynard. Gibson and Maynard were hardly young men when they started their second careers, nor were their thespic talents up to dealing with anything but the most rudimentary dialogue. But audiences generally preferred their heroes to be on the mature side, and they paid their money to see action and not acting. Thirteen years later Gibson and Maynard were still in the saddle, teaming up with Bob Steele in *Death Valley Rangers*, one of Monogram's Trail Blazer series. Gibson was in his fifties, worn and leathery; the 48-year-old Maynard's ample paunch, cascading over his belt, was a sad contrast to his athletic heyday in such early Universal talkies as *Mountain Justice* and *Sons of the Saddle.* In this company Bob Steele, at 37, was a relative youngster.

By the early 40s the popularity of these aging stars had been overshadowed by the likes of Don 'Red' Barry, Johnny Mack Brown and 'Wild Bill' Elliott. But they were all outlasted by one of the most durable of all action stars, William Boyd, Hopalong Cassidy of the Bar 20 Ranch.

A former leading man in Cecil B. De Mille silent spectaculars, Boyd's career was on the skids in 1935 when independent producer Harry Sherman offered him the part of Hopalong Cassidy, based on a character created by Clarence E. Mulford. Boyd had originally been earmarked to play the heavy in the series, but when the first choice for the lead, James Gleason, backed out, the part fell into the 40-year-old matinée idol's lap.

A poster promising 60 minutes of action-packed entertainment in George Sherman's 1938 *Three Texas Steers,* one of many Bs John Wayne made in the 30s – including some dubbed range warbling as Singin' Sandy in Monogram's *Riders of Destiny* (1933) – before he hit the jackpot in John Ford's *Stagecoach.*

71

In thirteen years there were 66 Cassidy adventures, 28 of which were directed by Lesley Selander: the experienced cameraman Russell Harlan photographed 44 of them, a remarkable tribute to the continuity of the Sherman production unit. The series gave the silver-haired Boyd the chance to create a memorably rounded Western hero, complete with twin-holsters and distinctive cowhead grip fastening his bandana; it brought Russell Hayden from behind the cameras and launched him on a career as a cowboy star; it enabled George 'Gabby' Hayes to perfect the character of the bewhiskered comic sidekick; and it introduced to the cinema a young actor with a laconic manner and interesting face — Robert Mitchum. Appearing initially as a bit-part heavy in *Hoppy Serves a Writ* in 1943, he soon moved on to more sympathetic parts before graduating to starring roles in RKO Bs *Nevada* and *West of the Pecos*.

The Hopalong Cassidy series was originally released by Paramount. In 1942 distribution was taken over by United Artists. Four years later Boyd bought the rights to the series and formed his own production company, but by then the best years were over, and the stresses and strains of plummeting budgets were plain to see. Late entries like *The Dead Don't Dream* were little more than feeble thrillers given a vaguely Western flavour and shot almost entirely indoors. It looked as if Boyd was washed up a second time but, as with Autry, television came to the rescue. The revival of the old Sherman features by NBC and a new series of 52 30-minute adventures restored Boyd's fortunes. He died, a rich man, in 1972.

The number of Hopalong Cassidy features is an indication of the voracious appetite of small-town American audiences for B Westerns. Another refugee from the silents, Johnny Mack Brown, appeared in 110 features in a Western career spanning twenty years. These movies were shot cheaply and fast by directors whose output was as prolific as those of the stars — William Witney, Lesley Selander, Lew Landers, Howard Bretherton, Derwin Abrahams, George Archainbaud, and Joseph Kane.

Kane's first directorial assignment, Republic's *Tumbling Tumbleweeds* (1935), made Gene Autry a star and launched a cycle of movies featuring cowboys who were as likely to reach for a guitar as a gun — Roy Rogers, Tex Ritter and, some way behind, Dick Foran, George Houston, Smith Ballew and Spectrum Pictures' Fred Scott, billed as 'The Silvery-Voiced Baritone'. *Tumbling Tumbleweeds* was shot in six days for the remarkably low sum, even by B movie standards, of $12,000. Kane went on to direct 17 more Autry pictures and then 43 with Roy Rogers. All were shot in six days on budgets which hovered around the $60,000 mark. Eventually Kane became both the producer and director of the Rogers pictures, making eight a year, each one taking about six weeks to complete. Kane's experience at Republic enabled him to transfer effortlessly to television in the late 50s, directing episodes of *Laramie, Bonanza* and *Cheyenne*. He once remarked that there was only one difference between films and television: at Republic you had to come up with 54 minutes in six days; on *Laramie* it was 48 minutes of story in five. However, first prize for speed must go to Yakima Canutt's 1953 *Outlaw Marshall*, a novelty Western which featured twenty stuntmen. In one frantic day's shooting the former stunt star managed no fewer than 87 set-ups.

Low budgets and tight schedules left many a Western more than a little frayed around the edges, particularly if it came from a rock-bottom independent like Reliable or Victory Pictures (an early enterprise of 50s schlockmeister Sam Katzman). Directors seldom allowed themselves the luxury of a retake. In PRC's *Frontier Outlaws* (1944) Buster Crabbe holds the villain at gunpoint while making his escape through a window, in the process giving his head a tremendous audible crack on the frame. Director Sam Newfield simply kept the cameras rolling. At the climax of *Westward Bound*, a 1944 Trail Blazers adventure, Hoot Gibson hurls a stick of

above
Tight-belted Hoot Gibson has to
be restrained in *The Boiling
Point* (1932), one of eleven
second-features the former
silent star made for H. H.
Hoffman's Allied Pictures in the
early 30s.

Ken Maynard at a temporary
disadvantage in Universal's 1933
Trail Drive.

Singing Cowboys

Durable Gene Autry, who launched the cycle with Republic's 1935 *Tumbling Tumbleweeds,* serenades Jean Heather, his co-star in *The Last Round-Up* (1947) directed by John English and Autry's first film for Columbia.

Roy Rogers and the Sons of the Pioneers in *Don't Fence Me In* (Republic, 1945) also directed by the hard-working English. The Sons of the Pioneers were (back row, l. to r.) Carl Farr, George 'Shug' Fisher, Hugh Farr; (front row, l. to r.) Ken Carson, Bob Nolan and Tim Spencer.

Universal's singing cowboy, well-laundered Bob Baker, in *The Last Stand* (1938), an oater given unaccustomed elegance by Joseph H. Lewis.

Old-timer Roscoe Ates eavesdropping on range warbler Eddie Dean and lovely Helen Mowery in PRC's *Range Beyond the Blue*.

Cannonball Taylor (on harmonica) and Jimmy Wakely (centre) in *Cowboy Cavalier* (1948), one of a series in which Monogram attempted to turn Country-and-Western singer Wakely into a poverty-row Gene Autry.

Ray Whitley, Tim Holt, Rita Hayworth and George O'Brien in *The Renegade Ranger*, a 1938 RKO Western. O'Brien, who had starred in Murnau's silent classic *Sunrise* in 1927, was nearly at the end of his career – he retired in 1940. Hayworth, still awaiting stardom, had already served time in Grand National's *Trouble in Texas* (1937) with singing cowboy Tex Ritter. Ray Whitley was a second-rank singing cowpoke who starred in his own RKO series of two-reelers.

Tom Keene defends his laundry in Monogram's *Painted Trail* (1938). Like many other sagebrush heroes who failed to last the distance, for example Wally Wales and Lane Chandler, Keene ended his career by playing heavies (as Richard Powers) in Tim Holt adventures at RKO, the studio which made Keene a B star in the early 30s. He also turned up in *Plan 9 From Outer Space* (1959).

Johnny Mack Brown lies doggo in Monogram's 1951 *Blazing Bullets*, while Dennis Moore and Stanley Price go about their villainous business. Like John Wayne, Mack Brown began his Western career with a big film – King Vidor's 1930 *Billy the Kid* – but never found a subsequent *Stagecoach*. This still finds him in an uncharacteristically supine mood – he was one of the Bs' supreme exponents of the punch-up.

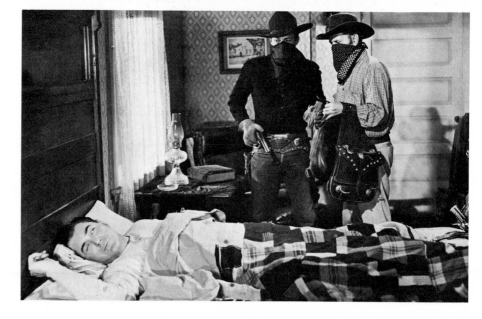

Texas Rangers Jimmy Dodd, Bob Steele and Tom Tyler admire the lacework in Republic's 1943 *Thundering Trails*, an episode in the final Three Mesquiteers series directed by John English. In all Republic ran 51 Mesquiteer features with nine different trio combinations. Both Tyler and Steele extended their range beyond Westerns. Tyler was Captain Marvel in the 1941 Republic serial *Adventures of Captain Marvel*; Steele played memorable non-Western roles in *Of Mice and Men* and *The Big Sleep*.

Wild Bill Elliott as Red Ryder having a few quiet words with his horse 'Thunder'. Doubtless he is telling Thunder that he's 'a peaceable man . . .'

left
Lash La Rue, king of the bullwhip, with his comic side-kick Al 'Fuzzy' St John in the PRC production *Cheyenne Takes Over* (1948). The Cheyenne tag was inherited from La Rue's previous appearance in several Eddie Dean adventures. A former hairdresser, La Rue was obviously not completely at home in the saddle or slugging it out with the likes of George Cheesebro, but the series still has its fans.

right
Allan 'Rocky' Lane temporarily separated from his horse 'Black Jack' in the 1950 *Covered Wagon Raid,* one of 38 tight little actioners he made for Republic between 1947 and 1953.

below left
A variegated crowd of extras look on as Dale Evans tends an unconscious Roy Rogers in the 1944 *San Fernando Valley.* In this film Roy received his first screen kiss – from Jean Porter in a dream sequence.

Psychological B Westerns.

above
Mary Stuart and William Bishop in Columbia's 1948 *Thunderhoof* direct by Phil Rosen. Along with Preston Foster they are on the trail of a legendary wild horse, 'Thunderhoof', a kind of B Western Moby Dick.

left
Barbara Bel Geddes, Bud Osborne and Tom Tully confront Robert Mitchum in Robert Wise's 1948 *Blood on the Moon.*

Rex Allen lashes out in *Thunder in God's Country* (Republic, 1951). A latecomer to the traditional B Western, Allen enjoyed an Indian Summer of popularity, making 19 features for Republic between 1950 and 1954. His last film for the studio was *Phantom Stallion*, directed by Harry Keller. Comic relief was initially provided by Buddy Ebsen and later Slim Pickens, with extra diversions from Koko the Wonder Horse. Allen was billed as the 'Arizona Cowboy' after his first starring feature of that name directed by R. G. Springsteen.

Joan Leslie in a tight spot in Alan Dwan's *The Woman They Almost Lynched* (Republic, 1953).

above left
Tim Holt and Richard Martin in RKO's 1948 *Gun Smugglers*, directed by Frank McDonald.

above right
Shapely female outlaw Virginia Mayo beats villain Stephen McNally to the draw in *Devil's Canyon* (1953), an RKO 3-D Western directed by Alfred Werker.

left
Macdonald Carey and Maureen O'Hara holding up a studio rock in George Sherman's *Commanche Territory* (1950), a biopic of Western scout Jim Bowie.

left
Beverly Tyler advises her
sweetheart Audie Murphy that
he should give himself up in
Cimarron Kid (1951) directed
by Budd Boetticher. Leif
Erickson (centre) looks on
grimly. Murphy, the most
decorated American soldier of
the Second World War, spent
most of his Hollywood career
confined to formula Westerns.

left
Every Western worth its salt
requires a hard-bitten belle of
the saloon. Marie Windsor fitted
the bill perfectly in Lesley
Selander's *Dakota Lil* (1950), in
which she had little difficulty in
appearing tougher than her co-
stars Rod Cameron and George
Montgomery.

above
Barbara Stanwyck as the queen
of Tombstone Territory in
Samuel Fuller's extraordinary
Forty Guns (1957), which boasts
more phallic imagery than the
facade of a Hindu temple.

dynamite at a gang of bandits; the stick thuds to the earth in full view of the audience while the special effects charges go off several yards away.

In the series format the liberal use of stock footage was inevitable, particularly as budgets dipped towards the end. The Lash La Rue films of the early 50s, produced by Ron Ormond's Western Adventure Productions, are often cited as the worst cases of a series cannibalizing itself. The 1951 *Thundering Trail* might well have been retitled *Thundering Library Shots*. Even the great Gene Autry was not immune. *The Last Round-Up* (1947) draws heavily on Wesley Ruggles' *Arizona* to liven up the action. At times a producer's efforts could seem almost archaeological. Warners' Brian Foy padded out singing cowboy Dick Foran's series with action footage from old Ken Maynard silents and even older Vitagraph material.

It was only a matter of time before a successful sequence was taken down from the shelf, dusted off and given a new home. The dramatic montage from Hopalong Cassidy's *Bar 20 Rides Again* (1935) in which Hoppy's ranch hands saddle up and gallop off to the rescue, was later used in several Cassidy adventures. Another feature in the series, *Rustler's Valley* (1937), climaxes with a spectacular rock slide. A 1942 remake, *Lost Canyon,* reused this sequence in its entirety, and one of the villains of an earlier movie, the young Lee J. Cobb, can clearly be seen.

Sometimes a complete movie was conjured up around some handy stock footage. In *Oklahoma Plains,* a 1952 Rex Allen for Republic, writer Milton Raison fashioned a slice of hokum about the early days of the tank around segments of B. Reeves 'Breezy' Eason's 1938 *Army Girl.*

It was not unusual for B Westerns to have a contemporary setting, although they were rarely as precisely dated as *Oklahoma Plains,* in which the action takes place in 1926. Rather they tended to inhabit a strange no-man's-land in which time is suspended halfway between the days of the old West and the 1940s. However, no one thought it remotely odd when their heroes shot back and forth like time travellers between the nineteenth and twentieth centuries. For example, *West of Cimmaron,* a 1941 Three Mesquiteers adventure set in the 1860s, was quickly followed by *Phantom Plainsmen* in which the Mesquiteers (Tom Tyler, Rufe Davies and Bob Steele) are hot on the trail of a Nazi agent.

During the Second World War the prairies swarmed with Nazis spies and saboteurs. Ken Maynard was quick off the mark in the 1939 *Death Rides the Range,* an early example of the wartime cowboys versus foreign agents adventure. In *Black Market Rustlers,* Range Busters Dennis Moore, Max Terhune and Ray 'Crash' Corrigan bring a gang of profiteers to book. An attempt was made to strike a note of social realism in *Raiders of Sunset Pass* (1943), one of Republic's ill-fated 'John Paul Revere' series; the plot revolved around a programme to alleviate the manpower shortage on the ranches by introducing cowgirls to the range. Strictly in the realm of fantasy was the 1944 *Moonlight and Cactus* in which the Andrews Sisters form an improbable trio of ranch hands. In Columbia's *Riders of the Northland* Charles Starrett and Cliff Edwards play two Texas rangers sent to Alaska to track down a gang of Nazi spies — another example of the time see-saw as the previous film in this Starrett series had been set in the early days of Texas.

A sizeable list could be made of B Westerns which attempted an exotic locale or an unusual plotline. *Hawaiian Buckaroo,* a 1937 Smith Ballew picture, kicks off in a pineapple plantation. In 1933, Buck Jones dealt with a bizarre religious sect in *Unknown Valley.* Twenty years later in *Desert Pursuit,* Wayne Morris and Virginia Grey were hunted across Death Valley by three gold-crazed Arabs; they are saved from death and worse by the intervention of a settlement of Californian Mission Indians. *Harlem on the Prairie* (1937) directed by Sam Newfield was billed as 'The World's First

Outdoor Action Adventure With An All-Negro Cast'. In Allan Dwan's 1953 *The Woman They Almost Lynched,* Audrey Totter and Joan Leslie face each other in one of the few female Western gun duels. The final shoot-out in Joseph H. Lewis' minimal 1958 Western, *Terror in a Texas Town,* pits a harpoon-wielding Swedish sailor played by Sterling Hayden against Ned Young's laid-back, black-garbed gunman. Nevertheless, audiences preferred the well-tried rituals of the half-dozen or so standard plot lines: cattlemen versus sodbusters; cattlemen versus rustlers; cattlemen versus cattlemen; the hoary old double role ploy with the innocent hero (more often than not Billy the Kid) being pursued for the misdeeds of a look-alike; and the fight to revenge the killing of parents, usually by a grasping cattle or railway baron.

A fine example of the last category is provided by *King of the Pecos* (1936), starring John Wayne in his pre-*Stagecoach* days and directed by Joseph Kane. Wayne avenges the murder of his parents by the evil cattle king 'Salamander' Styles, played with slimy brio by Cy Kendall, who is after a valuable waterhole on the edge of the desert. Excellent photography by Jack Marta and brisk, economical direction by Kane, keeps the film cracking along at a breakneck pace. Intervals of comic relief are supplied by two old-timers and love interest is provided by Muriel Evans. There are well-orchestrated chase sequences and a final showdown in the rocks, where Kendall bites the dust. The regular appearance of familiar heavies like Kendall, Tristram Coffin, George Cheesebro, Fred Kohler, Wheeler Oakman and Roy Barcroft, who was equally at home as villainous railway baron or unshaven outlaw, provided another essential element in a self-perpetuating cycle. The culminating violence in which they invariably received their just deserts fell some way short of blood-soaked *Wild Bunch* standards, but occasionally a more sombre note was struck. An abiding image of the Roy Rogers *Far Frontier* is that of Barcroft callously dumping oil barrels containing smuggled aliens into a lake. In *Bells of San Angelo* (1947) you could sense the audience wincing as Rogers received a terrific battering from a couple of outlaws played by ace stuntmen Dale Van Sickel and David Sharpe.

From time to time issues which are fashionable today were crammed into the 60-minute compass of a horse opera. Tex Ritter's *Where the Buffalo Roam* (1938), shed a quick tear for the wanton destruction of the great buffalo herds before moving onto the song numbers. The excellent Fred Myton script in *White Eagle,* directed by Lambert Hillyer in 1932, allowed Buck Jones to lament the exploitation of Indians.

Another veteran of the silents, Buck Jones was one of the most popular cowboy heroes of the early 30s. Strong and silent in the William S. Hart mould, he also had a streak of self-deprecating humour which on occasion led him to adopt highly unconvincing Mexican disguises in adventures set south of the border. Another old timer, Tim McCoy, also resorted to this device. However, by 1941 when they were paired in the Monogram Rough Riders series, they were sensibly leaving the Latin stuff to the likes of Cesar Romero, Gilbert Roland, and Duncan Renaldo.

For Western thrills Republic rose head and shoulders above the other studios. Gene Autry was their first big star. By 1947 the Republic lot had become too small for both Autry and Roy Rogers, and Autry moved on to Columbia, leaving Rogers behind as King of the Cowboys. Republic also developed the most popular of the trio Westerns, the Three Mesquiteers series. The first Republic Mesquiteers feature was released in 1936, with Ray 'Crash' Corrigan, Robert Livingston and Syd Saylor respectively, playing the roles of Tuscon Smith, Stony Brooke and Lullaby. The following seven years saw the production of 51 Mesquiteer films with nine different combinations of the trio. In 1938-9 John Wayne appeared as Stoney Brooke in eight adventures, the most enjoyable of which was *Three Texas Steers,* a

Two Budd Boetticher films from the 'Ranown' cycle, an acronym derived from the names of Randolph Scott (star and associate producer) and Harry Joe Brown (executive producer) who combined to produce an interesting series of low budget Westerns in the 50s.

left
Randolph Scott and Craig Stevens in *Buchanan Rides Alone* (1958).

below
Karen Steele, Scott and his prisoner James Best in *Ride Lonesome* (1959).

good example of the distance which oaters could travel from traditional Western plot lines. Wayne and his companions, Robert Livingston and Max Terhune, save Carole Landis' circus from the clutches of its fraudulent manager. There's a gorilla (or rather a man in a gorilla suit) terrorizing Terhune, and a circus dancing horse which breaks into one of its big-top routines in the middle of a vital trotting race. The horse is smuggled to the race track in a covered wagon pulled by a military halftrack, commandeered out of thin air by Max Terhune, a strange juxtaposition of modern technology and echoes of the past.

As the Mesquiteers series was coming to an end, 'Wild Bill' Elliott joined Republic from Columbia, reviving the 'Red Ryder' role made popular in the early 40s by Don Barry. Bobby Blake, a sympathetic child actor, played the part of the Little Beaver, his small Indian sidekick. As an adult, and something of a veteran, Robert Blake was to star in *In Cold Blood* and *Electra Glide in Blue*. Stern and steady as a rock, 'Wild Bill' is remembered with great affection for the oft-repeated drawl, 'I'm a peaceable man but . . .' as he reluctantly readied himself to pummel stock Republic heavies Roy Barcroft, Bud Geary and Kenne Duncan into the dust.

The Republic Westerns were manufactured by a small army of highly efficient technicians: directors like William Witney, George Sherman and John English; cameramen Jack Marta, William Bradford and Bud Thackery; brilliant stuntmen of the calibre of Yakima Canutt (later a director of B Westerns), Tom Steele and Duke Greene; and a band of hard-working musical supervisors, with Mort Glickman outstanding, composing a stream of stirring scores for the studio's 40-piece orchestra.

Republic's great days were long over when in January 1959 the studio released its final picture. Appropriately it was a B Western, *Plunderers of Painted Flats*, starring Corinne Calvert, John Carroll, Skip Homeier, George Macready and Edmund Lowe. Filmed in black and white and lasting 77 minutes, it fell back on the old 'revenge for my father's killing' plot.

The same year also saw the release of *Ride Lonesome*, the penultimate in a series of low-budget Westerns starring Randolph Scott and directed by Budd Boetticher, which over the years have attracted considerable critical attention. Although their individual budgets would have funded an entire PRC Buster Crabbe series of the 40s, they nevertheless fall into the B category, their austere settings and sparse scripting — four of them by Burt Kennedy — giving them a style and self-assurance superior to many A Westerns of the period. *Seven Men From Now, Decision At Sundown, Ride Lonesome* and *Commanche Station* are all 'revenge' Westerns, with Scott a grim and lonely figure seeking justice for the killing of his wife. The changing landscape across which he travels is inhabited by a shifting population of drifters and outlaws — vividly etched by such excellent character actors as Henry Silva, Richard Boone and Lee Marvin — with whom Scott often finds himself in uneasy and temporary alliance.

Randolph Scott's weathered charm and Boetticher's confident direction, with its emphasis on clean, Fordian lines give these modest films a remarkable feeling of unity. No such distinction can be claimed for the A. C. Lyles Bs of the 60s. Directed by seasoned hands Leslie Selander and R. G. Springsteen, such programmers as *Town Tamer* and *Apache Uprising* plodded down well-worn trails. What they did have in common, apart from a decided lack of production values, was a battalion of movie veterans who had seen better days, an indication of Lyles' early career as a publicist. Pressed into service to give some nostalgia value, if not life, to the series were Bruce Cabot, Richard Arlen, John Agar, Lon Chaney, Wendell Cory, Barton Maclane, Johnny Mack Brown, Lyle Bettger, Coleen Gray, Yvonne de Carlo and the egregious Sonny Tufts, a sad epitaph, if ever there was one, to the B Western.

above
One of the strangest showdowns in the history of the B Western. Harpoon-wielding Sterling Hayden faces up to Ned Young in Joseph H. Lewis' final film *Terror in a Texas Town* (1958), shot in ten days for a mere $80,000. No prizes for guessing who wins.

above left
Betsy Blair in Joseph H. Lewis' *The Halliday Brand* (1957), a routine assignment – the story of Joseph Cotten's revolt against his tyrannical father (Ward Bond) – given considerable resonance by Lewis' eloquent direction.

left
Yvonne de Carlo offers John Ireland a new hat in the 1967 A. C. Lyles production *Arizona Bushwackers* directed by Lesley Selander. Other veterans in the cast were Howard Keel, Scott Brady, Brian Donlevy and James Craig.

QUICK, IGOR! THE SHOVEL
HORRORS

Horror is the most adaptable of film genres. Lycanthropy can lurk in the antiseptic environment of a high school or the deep-piled corridors of the White House. Count Dracula has strayed a long way from Transylvania, seeking nourishment on the prairies of the West and the tenements of the East Side. Since 1931 battallions of man-made monsters, the grandchildren of Rabbi Judah Low Ben Bezalel and Dr Frankenstein, have levered themselves off the laboratory table and lumbered out of their spark-filled quarters to celebrate their brief, doomed existence. Brains, hands, hearts and eyes have been transplanted in the strangest of circumstances, inevitably with depressing results for all concerned. Zombies from all walks of life have plodded around, looking frightful but usually doing little harm, although in recent years they have developed a distressing taste for human flesh.

The immense success in 1931 of James Whale's *Frankenstein* and Todd Browning's *Dracula* was not lost on the men who ran Hollywood's B units. It was ironic, therefore, that as the popularity of the horror film began to wane, the two stars of these classics, Boris Karloff and Bela Lugosi, found their way into low-budget productions. In 1936, with *The Man They Could Not Hang*, Karloff embarked on a long stint of 'Mad Doctor' roles for Columbia. Directed by Nick Grinde, Karloff played Dr Henryk Savaard who is revived by his own invention, a mechanical heart, after being hanged for murder. Mad Doctors usually fall victim to their own experiments, and Karloff was no exception. In *The Man With Nine Lives* (1940), he emerges from a ten-year deep freeze only to become totally unhinged by the experience. In the same year in *Before I Hang*, a serum concocted from the blood of a murdered young man is injected into Karloff's ailing heart. Alas, there are unlooked for side effects: the young man was a murderer and his 'bad blood' sends Karloff away on a strangling rampage. In Edward Dmytryk's *The Devil Commands* (1941), Karloff's obsessive desire to communicate with his dead wife from his private power station inevitably leads to disaster. The Columbia series ended in 1942 with broad comedy — Lew Landers' *The Boogie Man Will Get You* — in which Karloff and Peter Lorre attempt to turn slapstick comic Maxie Rosenbloom into a superman in the basement of Jeff Donnell's hotel.

Boris Karloff was a fine actor and well able to emerge with at least some shreds of dignity still intact from such farragos as *Abbott and Costello Meet Frankenstein* (1948). The reserved and immensely professional Englishman always took a touch of self-deprecating humour with him onto the set. Edgar Ulmer recalled that when directing Karloff in *The Black Cat*

Two of Bela Lugosi's best roles of the 30s.

left
As Dr Vitus Verdegast in Edgar Ulmer's 1934 *The Black Cat,* he is about to flay alive the equally improbably named Hjalmar Poelzig (Boris Karloff).

below left
Lugosi as the supposedly blind Dr Orloff in the British *Dark Eyes of London* (1939), an Edgar Wallace story directed by Walter Summers. Hugh Williams is the natty gent and Wilfred Walter Lugosi's blind, disfigured underling.

below
Mad doctor at work. Lionel Atwill as Dr Otto van Niemann of Kleinschloss working on a blood substitute to transfuse into the veins of unsuspecting Fay Wray in *The Vampire Bat* (1933).

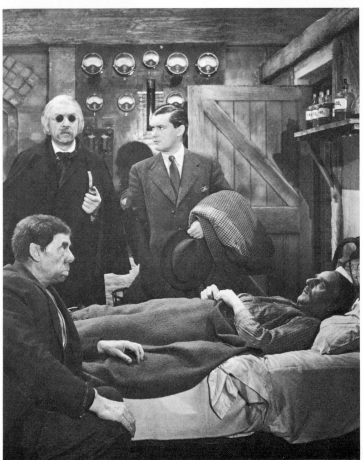

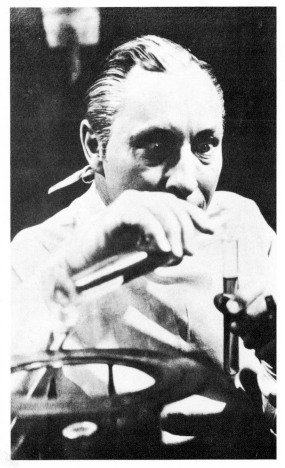

89

(1934), 'Every time I had him come in by the door, he would open the door and say "Here comes the heavy" '. Lugosi, on the other hand, was at bottom a terrible ham — in *The Black Cat* Ulmer had constantly to cut away from the Hungarian actor in order to keep his performance in some kind of proportion. His thick Hungarian accent also made him difficult to cast, and after his great triumph as Dracula his career rapidly entered a downward spiral. Throughout the 30s Lugosi still managed to secure parts in interesting films — Victor Halperin's *White Zombie* (1932), Lew Landers' *The Raven* (1935) and Lambert Hillyer's *The Invisible Ray* (1936) — but although he retained his star billing the parts grew smaller, and by the early 40s he was down among the dead men in PRC productions like *The Devil Bat* (1940). Further indignities lay in store for Lugosi, now in the grip of a drug addiction that by the end of his life had filled his body with a collection of substances probably more outlandish than those required to animate Frankenstein's monster: *Zombies on Broadway* (1945), *Mother Riley Meets the Vampire* (1952), *Bride of the Monster* (1956) and, posthumously, *Plan 9 From Outer Space* (1959). The last, released three years after his death, contains some brief, pathetic shots of the shrunken star doddering around his home, and about thirty seconds of Lugosi in his Dracula kit. Director Edward Wood Jnr spliced this footage into his grade Z classic about Grave Robbers from Outer Space. Wood eked out the Lugosi footage with a 'double' who attempts to disguise the fact by stumbling around with is face buried in his cape. The result was promoted as 'The Great Bela Lugosi's last film'.

By 1937 the momentum was running out of the first horror cycle and there was a two-year gap in which none of the major studios released a horror film. Universal reissued *Dracula* and *Frankenstein* in 1938 and the box-office returns prompted them to relaunch the horror film in the following year with Rowland V. Lee's stylish homage to Expressionism, *Son of Frankenstein*. Next to return to the screen was The Invisible Man in *The Invisible Man Returns* (1940), directed by Joe May with Vincent Price as the transparent one. Two low-budget sequels completed the mini-series, *The Invisible Agent* (1942), an improbable wartime adventure in which vanishing Jon Hall parachutes into Berlin, and *The Invisible Man's Revenge* (1944), with Hall recovering his anti-social tendencies and transfusing John Carradine's blood into his own veins in order to regain visibilty.

Universal's formula for horror films in the 40s consisted of little more than throwing together B versions of their triumphs of the previous decade. Every expense was spared in *The Mummy's Hand*, an extremely cost-conscious sequel to Karl Freund's *The Mummy* (1932), which provided Universal with one of their most profitable films of 1940. The temple master-set in *The Mummy's Hand* was lifted wholesale from James Whale's jungle-expedition epic *Green Hell*, and the explanatory flashbacks come from the Karloff film. Dick Foran, Wallace Ford, Peggy Moran and Cecil Kellaway form a somewhat unlikely archaeological team on the trail of the tomb of the Egyptian princess Ananka. Instead, they unearth Kharis, Ananka's mummy guardian, kept alive over the centuries with a diet of tanna leaves administered by the High Priests of Karnak, the latest incumbent being silky-smooth villain George Zucco, a professor at Cairo Museum. Stepping up the dosage of tanna leaves, Zucco sets the mute mummy (his tongue was cut out when he was buried alive) on the profane archaeologists. Arab guide Leon Belasco and professor Charles Trowbridge are swiftly throttled while Zucco hatches a plan to take a tanna-fuelled trip into eternity with pretty Peggy Moran. Dick Foran shoots him before he can administer the fatal brew, and his bandaged minion is set ablaze by a toppling brazier.

The Mummy's Hand set the tone of the following films. *The Mummy's Tomb* (1942) not only used flashbacks footage from its 1940 predecessor but also cannibalized the village mob sequence from *Frankenstein*. Zucco turned up again in *The Mummy's Tomb* — apparently Foran's fusillade of shots had only succeeded in 'crushing' his arm — and again in *The Mummy's Ghost*, handing on the secret of the tanna leaves to John Carradine. In *The Mummy's Hand* the big Band-Aid monster was played by former cowboy star Tom Tyler. In the subsequent films, including *The Mummy's Curse* (1944), Universal make-up man Jack Pierce devoted hours to winding yards of bandaging around Universal's new horror star, Lon Chaney Jnr.

As Creighton Chaney, son of The Man of a Thousands Faces Lon Chaney, the hulking actor had knocked around for years in small parts, finally attracting critical attention in 1939 as the retarded Lennie in Lewis Milestone's *Of Mice and Men*. His performance in the following year as the one-eyed Akhoba, the brutal leader of the Rock People in Hal Roach's *One Million BC*, led to a contract with Universal and a publicity build-up which aimed at, but never succeeded in, putting him in his father's shoes.

Chaney's first film for Universal, *Man-Made Monster*, was only a qualified success. He played a carnival sideshow attraction, The Electrical Man, who falls into the clutches of crazed scientist Lionel Atwill. Boosted with huge electrical charges, including a massive shock from the electric chair which leaves him a pulsating, high-voltage monster, Chaney finally meets his end when his protective rubber suit snags on a barbed wire fence.

At Universal Chaney went on to play the complete range of movie monsters: Frankenstein's creation in *The Ghost of Frankenstein* (1942); Count Dracula in *Son of Dracula* (1943); and the lycanthrope Larry Talbot in *The Wolf Man* (1941), *Frankenstein Meets the Wolf Man* (1943) and *House of Frankenstein* (1944). (The last two films, with their contrived encounters between the studio's monsters, anticipate the riotous Godzilla free-for-alls in the 1960s.)

Chaney also starred in a series of Bs lumped together under the name of The Inner Sanctum mysteries. Based on a successful radio programme they were brisk little tales of the supernatural, the best of which was *Weird Woman* (1944). The film gave Evelyn Ankers — usually on the receiving end of Chaney's monstrous attentions — a chance to play a witch, jilted by Chaney's rather unconvincing college professor and determined to use the black arts to dispose of his new wife, Anne Gwynne. The tables are turned on her by spooky Elizabeth Russell, the widow of one of Ankers' previous victims. Letting rip with one of her celebrated screams, Ankers goes crazy, topples off a roof and, for good measure, hangs herself from a grapevine. Adapted from a Fritz Leiber story, *Weird Woman* was remade in 1962 as *Burn Witch Burn*, a genuinely frightening film directed by Sidney Hayers, and starring Janet Blair and Peter Wyngarde.

Chaney was never a convincing successor to Karloff and Lugosi. He remained an actor of extremely limited range trapped in the shadow of his father's reputation and fixated by his one truly original interpretation, Lennie in *Of Mice and Men*. Director Reginald LeBorg, who knew him well (and directed him in *The Mummy's Ghost, Calling Dr Death, Weird Woman* and *Dead Man's Eyes*) recalled that many years later when working on *The Black Sleep* (1956), Chaney was still using the shuffling gait he had devised for *The Wolf Man* and the inarticulate grunts and grimaces of the subnormal Lennie.

In the horror Bs of the 40s the acting (or over-acting) honours invariably went to the rich crop of mad doctors whose laboratories heaved with the ghastly results of their botched experiments. In *The Mad Ghoul* (1945) George Zucco, on the track of an ancient life-preserving process turns assistant David Bruce into a corpse-like zombie who requires an endless series of heart transplants to keep him tottering about on his boss' evil business. Finally Zucco inhales his own deadly gas and instantly becomes a ghoul himself. We leave him in his death throes, scrabbling feebly at a grave in a desperate attempt to secure a new heart. In PRC's *The Mad Monster* (1941) Zucco pumps odd-job man Glenn Strange full of wolf's blood in an attempt to turn him into a controllable superman, but instead ends up on the receiving end of an uncontrollable wolf man. In Stuart Heisler's *The Monster and the Girl* (1941) Zucco transfers murderer Philip Terry's brain into an ape which then lumbers off to wreak revenge on the men who sent Terry to the chair.

The frenetic scientific activities of Zucco and his confrères, the cadaverous John Carradine and the intense Lionel Atwill, give new meaning to the notion of 'winning hearts and minds'. Monogram took note and teamed Zucco and Carradine with Bela Lugosi in William Beaudine's *Voodoo Man* (1944) and then put them through their paces in *Return of the Ape Man,* in which Carradine becomes a reluctant brain donor to mixed-up neanderthal man George Zucco.

The Monogram and PRC lots may well have been pullulating with the victims of these over-enthusiastic transplant pioneers, but at RKO's B horror unit producer Val Lewton put his signature on a very different approach. In Fox's *The Undying Monster* (1942), John Brahm had already shown what could be achieved with mood and suggestion. Lewton, saddled by his boss Charles Koerner with arbitrary and corny titles like *Cat People* and *I Walked with a Zombie,* produced a series of delicately wrought chillers which relied on atmosphere, on our fear of the unseen, to achieve their effect. Around him Lewton assembled a formidable team: Jacques Tourneur, who directed *Cat People* (1942), *I Walked with a Zombie* (1943) and *The Leopard Man* (1943); Robert Wise, director of *Curse of the Cat People* (1944) and *The Body Snatcher* (1945); Mark Robson, who edited the first three Lewton/Tourneur films and then went on to direct *The Seventh Victim, Ghost Ship, Isle of the Dead* and *Bedlam*; screenwriter De Witt Bodeen and cameraman Nick Musuraca. Over the work of these talented collaborators hangs the sophisticated, literary organizing intelligence of Lewton. As he remarked, when recalling *I Walked with a Zombie,* 'it was turned into Jane Eyre in the West Indies'. Occasionally a literary conceit was slightly overworked; in *The Seventh Victim,* the use of the closing line of a Donne sonnet, 'I run to Death, and Death meets me as fast, and all my Pleasures are like Yesterdays', is in the context more than a little pretentious. Nevertheless, Lewton's films are perhaps the outstanding examples of the creative handling of the perennial B limitations — low budgets, standing sets, contract players, trite storylines — and the highly individual stamp a brilliant producer can leave on a series of films, a salutary corrective to the habit of thinking solely in terms of directors. Above all, the films have left a series of haunting images which once experienced are never forgotten. The moonlight walk through the rustling cane fields in *I Walked with a Zombie*; Jean Brooks in *The Seventh Victim* slumped in an armchair and surrounded by a coven of Devil worshippers willing her drink from the poisoned cup set before her; the brilliantly timed shock as a New York bus' doors hiss open to offer Jane Randolph refuge from her deadly, unseen pursuer in *Cat People.*

The subtle enchantments of Val Lewton did not drive away the mad doctors, and in the 50s they made a remarkable comeback. In the 40s there was little heed taken of the wider context of scientific responsibility. Crazed scientists shot you full of wolf's blood, or crammed ape's brains into your cranium, because that was what crazed scientists did. In the 50s their activities took place in the queasy moral climate of the nuclear age and occasionally required qualification, however, perfunctory. As a result there were a number of gallant attempts to locate the traditional elements of the horror film in a new landscape. Radioactivity became the convenient

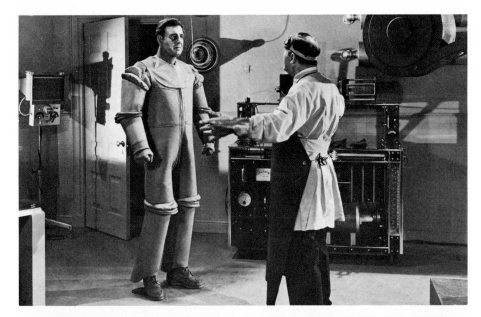

Lon Chaney Jnr in his first horror role for Universal. Charged with thousands of volts of electricity, and modelling the latest thing in rubber wear, he lumbers towards Lionel Atwill in *Man-Made Monster* (1941).

The fog machine working overtime at the climax of George Waggner's *The Wolf Man* (Universal, 1941). Claude Rains is about to dispatch Lon Chaney with a silver-topped cane. Evelyn Ankers has understandably been overcome by all the excitement.

George Zucco contemplates taking tanna leaves for two with helpless Peggy Moran on the master set for Christy Cabanne's *The Mummy's Hand* (1940), originally built for James Whale's jungle drama *Green Hell*. Western star Tom Tyler is the man concealed beneath several hundred yards of bandages.

above
Universal did not possess the monopoly on horror Bs, or of improbable plots. In Paramount's 1941 *The Monster and the Girl*, directed by Stuart Heisler, an ape is given condemned man Phillip Terry's brain by George 'they call me a scientist' Zucco.

above right
Bela Lugosi turned down the role of Frankenstein's monster in James Whale's 1931 classic but twelve years later he was grateful for the part in Universal's *Frankenstein Meets the Wolf Man* (1943) directed by Roy William Neill, with a screenplay by Curt Siodmak. Lon Chaney was the Wolf Man.

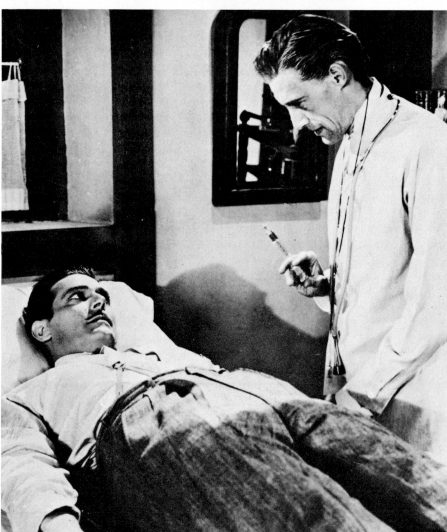

right
Jon Hall looks apprehensive as John Carradine brandishes the syringe in Universal's *The Invisible Man's Revenge* (1944) directed by Ford Beebe.

Abbott and Costello Meet Dr Jekyll and Mr Hyde (1953), the penultimate port of call in the comedy duo's voyage around Hollywood's monsters. The last in the series was *Abbott and Costello Meet the Mummy* (1955). At least the Creature from the Black Lagoon had the good taste to avoid the Abbott and Costello treatment.

Bela Lugosi in uncharacteristically restrained mood between John McGuire and Polly Ann Young in Joseph H. Lewis' *The Invisible Ghost*, a 1941 Sam Katzman Banner film for Monogram.

Bela Lugosi and John Carradine are nonplussed by George Zucco's neanderthal man in PRC's 1944 *Return of the Ape Man*, directed by Phil Rosen.

right
Lon Chaney Jnr and Evelyn
Ankers in Universal's 1944
Weird Woman, an 'Inner
Sanctum' mystery directed by
Reginald LeBorg.

Restraint, atmosphere and an undeniably literary approach characterized producer Val Lewton's horror Bs for RKO.

bottom left
Kent Smith, Jane Randolph, Eve March, Elizabeth Russell and Julia Dean at the climax of *Curse of the Cat People* (1944). Ostensibly a sequel to *Cat People*, it was a haunting meditation on the poetry and danger of childhood in the style of *Turn of the Screw.*

right
Francis Dee and Christine Gordon in *I Walked with a Zombie* (1943).

centre right
The coven of Palladists willing Jean Brooks to drain the poisoned glass in *The Seventh Victim* (1943).

bottom right
Karloff and Lugosi in *The Bodysnatcher* (made in 1943 but not released until 1945).

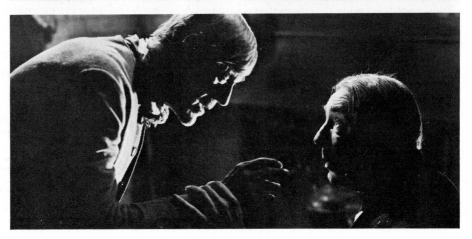

'I'm terribly interested in the mind.'

left
Otto Kruger prepares to transfer ape woman Amelita Ward's brain into Vicky Lane's cranium in *Jungle Captive* (1944) directed by Harold Young. The sinister figure on the right is Rondo Hatton.

below left
Lew Ayres is falling into the grip of *Donovan's Brain* (1953) directed by Felex Feist. This Curt Siodmak story has also been filmed as *The Lady and the Monster* and *The Brain*.

below right
Joseph Evers tends his decapitated fiancée in *The Brain That Wouldn't Die* (1962).

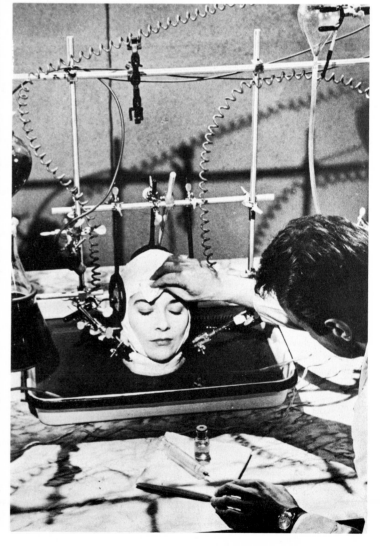

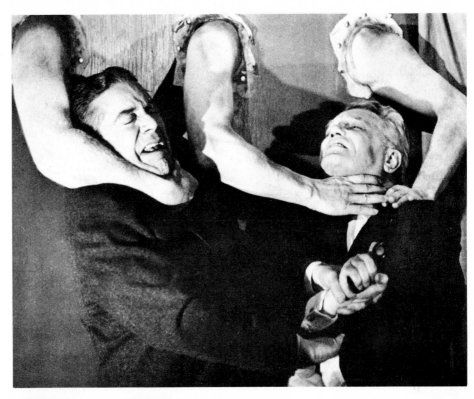

right
Nazi neurosurgeon Dana
Andrews comes to a sticky end
in *The Frozen Dead* (1967).

below left
Karen Parker's brain being
drained by materialized thought
in *Fiend Without a Face* (1958).

below right
The somewhat less than
convincing result of imaginative
surgery by Bruce Dern in AIP's
*The Incredible Two-Headed
Transplant* (1971); retarded John
Bloom is on the left and
homicidal maniac Albert Cole
on the right.

above
Nils Asther and Reinhold Schunzel in Ralph Murphy's *The Man in Half Moon Street* (1944). They are both the same age – Asther has preserved his youth by regular gland transplants performed by Schunzel. The film was remade by Hammer in 1959 as *The Man Who Could Cheat Death* with Anton Diffring in Asther's role.

above left
Andrea King finds a wandering hand in Robert Florey's *The Beast With Five Fingers* (1947). The hand used to belong to a concert pianist but takes on a sinister life of its own when the virtuoso dies, crawling around and putting in a few stints of strangulation as an agreeable alternative to Bach. This is one of Luis Bûnuel's favourite films.

A race of troglodytes emerges from beneath the Himalayas to menace explorer John Agar and his companions in Virgil Vogel's *The Mole People* (1956).

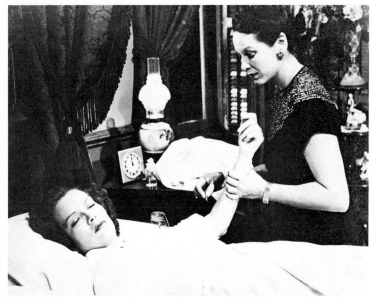

above
Susan Cabot on the track of the elixir of youth in Roger Corman's 1959 *Wasp Woman*. As the title suggests, the new wonder drug has unfortunate side effects.

above right
Gale Sondergaard has an arterial motive in drawing out the blood from Brenda Joyce in *The Spider Woman Strikes Back* (Universal, 1946) directed by Arthur Lubin.

right
Richard Crane has an unattractive skin condition in *The Alligator People*. Beverly Garland is his long-suffering wife. Roy Del Ruth directed this 1959 cheapie.

Scientist Robert Shayne's experiments turned him into a missing link in *The Neanderthal Man*, directed by E. A. Dupont in 1953.

Zombies have always been popular with B horror producers, who are eager to fill the screen with non-speaking actors.

top right
Death advances by geometrical progression in George Romero's *Night of the Living Dead* (1968).

left
Victor Halperin's Gothic *White Zombie* (1932): Bela Lugosi (far right) as Haitian zombie master Murder Legendre has Madge Bellamy and Robert Frazer in his power while John Harron watches in horror from the staircase.

left
Less successful was Halperin's *Revolt of the Zombies* (1936) in which a regiment of Indo-Chinese walking dead go over the top in the First World War.

left
John Gilling's *The Plague of the Zombies*, an above-average Hammer film of 1966.

below
Michael Landon as the hyperactive high school student in Herman Cohen's *I Was a Teenage Werewolf* (1957).

left
Deaf-and-dumb Judith Evelyn gets the chop in William Castle's *The Tingler* (1959). A form of materialized terror is growing at the base of her spine in the shape of a crab-like parasite. Removed in an autopsy by scientist Vincent Price, the scuttling monster escapes into a cinema, at which point selected members of the audience were given a mild shock by specially wired seats.

Hammer Horrors

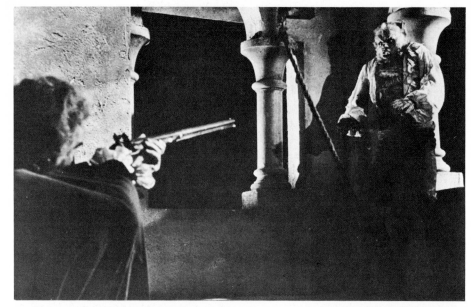

Oliver Reed as the hairy one gets the silver bullet in the 1961 *Curse of the Werewolf.*

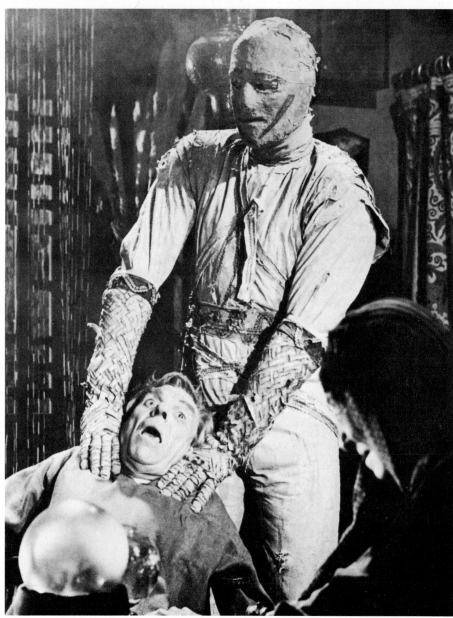

André Morell seems to be dying of fright rather than any pressure applied by Christopher Lee in *The Mummy* (1959). Attempting to fill the shoes of Universal's master of make-up Jack Pierce was Hammer's Phil Leakey.

agent of transformation. In *Creature with the Atom Brain* (1955), Edward L. Cahn contrived an uneasy marriage of the Frankenstein and Zombie themes with fanciful B notions of the new technology. Steve Ritchie, turns into a lycanthrope in Fred Sears' *The Werewolf* (1956) after scientists inject him with a serum to combat radiation poisoning. In *The Vampire* (1957) atom experiments turn scientist John Beal into a bloodsucker.

Unconventional methods of brain surgery remained popular, however. In *The Brain That Wouldn't Die* (1963), surgeon Joseph Evers attempts to keep his girlfriend alive after she has been decapitated in an auto accident. Hooking her head up to an assortment of bubbling test tubes, and leaving it to marinate in a chemical-filled tray, he sets off to cruise the local bars for a suitably attractive body to attach to what remains of his fiancée. The anguished head succeeds in willing one of Evers' failed experiments from a closet in the lab. The 'thing' rips off Evers' assistant's one good arm (in a gruesome scene the wretched man reels around the lab, smearing blood all over the walls) and then begins to eat Evers as they all go up in flames. One wonders if the final moments in which the 'thing' starts tucking into its tormentor influenced Romero's *Night of the Living Dead*.

Even more farfetched was *The Man Without a Body* (1957), in which a spirited attempt was made to revive and communicate with the head of seventeenth-century sage Nostradamus. In *The Frozen Dead* (1967) ex-Nazi scientist Dana Andrews instals a disembodied head in his lab in a desperate bid to accelerate his defrosting experiments on a small army of Hitler's deep-frozen finest. (Edward Fox has a 'non-speaking' part as his zombie brother, victim of an over-hasty retrieval from the refrigerator.) As Dana's ultra-sophisticated revival process seems to consist of jabbing his patients in the neck with a large knitting needle, the failure rate is understandably high. But 'Zere iz no room for miztakes', as a visiting Nazi bigwig insists, and he presses relentlessly on. Once again the anguished head brings about his end — he is strangled by a hedge of disembodied arms to which the brain is connected.

These scientific disasters pale in comparison with those of the most accomplished of all postwar mad doctors, Whit Bissell, the creator of the teenage werewolf and Frankenstein monster. In turn, they were the creation of a young entrepreneur Herman Cohen who, in a flash of brilliance, grafted two classic elements of the horror film on to the teen agony movie to give the waiting world in 1957, *I Was a Teenage Werewolf* and *I Was a Teenage Frankenstein*.

Why does pensive Michael Landon, star student at Rockdale High School, fly into tantrums at the slightest provocation? Why has he started to eat his hamburgers raw? Sinister psychologist Whit Bissell has the answer – 'There are certain tell-tale marks on his body only I can recognize', he tells his assistant, as with the help of a serum he prepares to hurl the youth back to his 'primitive state', apparently to give the human race a fresh start. The result, a teenage werewolf who sprouts hair and fangs every time the class bell rings. In the same year Bissell and Cohen teamed up again to produce *I Was a Teenage Frankenstein* in which Whit, a representative of an American cadet branch of the Frankenstein family, assembles a teenage monster (Gary Conway) from spare parts provided by dead hot rodders. 'He's crying, even the tear ducts work' he exults over his new creation. The success of Cohen's films led to a crop of cheap imitators: *Teenage Monster, Teenage Zombies* and Roger Corman's *Teenage Caveman*, in which 26-year-old Robert Vaughan looked a trifle long in the tooth for the lead role.

Far more amusing, and effective, was the tongue-in-cheek *A Bucket of Blood* (1959), with Dick Miller as a beat sculptor whose manifest lack of talent leads him to take a short-cut to a new form of social realism. He builds his sculptures around the bodies of a succession of murder victims. When his secret is revealed, he decides on artistic self-immolation, coating himself with clay and hanging himself. The film moves in one of Corman's favourite locales of the late 50s, the world of 'beatnik' coffee bars, hep-cats and flamboyant but small-time entrepreneurs in shades and black roll-necks, with huge medallions hanging from their necks, talking in machine-gun bursts of insane jive talk.

While Rockdale High School was being convulsed by a series of inexplicable murders, in England a small independent studio, Hammer, released *The Curse of Frankenstein*, the first in their long line of films which re-explored the territory abandoned by Universal in the late 40s. It is debatable whether the Hammer films fall into the B category covered by this book. Nevertheless, their output represents the natural successor to the Universal films and as such merits some attention. The films are characterized by a familiar stock company of stars (Peter Cushing, Christopher Lee) and a gallery of character actors whose appearance serves as convenient plot shorthand. Especially memorable is pop-eyed little Michael Ripper, usually playing the gormless yokel who provides the monster with its first victim. Such familiarity can become grating. The constant reappearance of the same master-set as Castle Dracula or Baskerville Hall underlines the stodginess and lack of imagination that lies at the heart of the Hammer films. The worst offender is director Terence Fisher, who for some inexplicable reason has been extravagantly lauded by French critics. There are, it is true, some visually arresting moments in Fisher's films, but these often owe more to the production designer than the director: Christopher Lee's Mummy emerging from a bubbling Dartmoor tarn in a landscape of lurid, almost psychedelic, brilliance remains long in the mind. However, compared with the stylized elegance of such films as Rowland V. Lee's *Son of Frankenstein* (art director, Jack Otterson) Fisher's over-lit, over-upholstered productions, with their sluggish pace and banal direction, are disappointing successors to the Universal tradition. With some notable exceptions, even the bit-part regulars lack the bravura touch, invarably supplied by Universal contract players like Maria Ouspenskaya and Eduardo Cianelli.

Hammer provided more blood and gratuitous shocks than Universal, but their effects seem postively restrained when compared with the tidal wave of gore washing through films of fringe producer/directors like Ted V. Mikels *(The Astro Zombies, The Corpse Grinders)* and the outrageous Herschell Gordon Lewis, whose output included *Blood Feast, Gruesome Twosome, Wizard of Gore, Two Thousand Maniacs!* and *Gore-Gore Girls.* In these blood-boltered epics of the 60s and early 70s, Lewis' dismally amateur actors wade through banks of human offal on their way from one desembowelling to the next. As the great director proudly announced, 'Peckinpah's blood is much more watery than ours, Peckinpah shoots people. We dismember them!' Connoisseurs of the genre will recall the moment in *Blood Feast* when a young girl, in the ultimate non-speaking part, has her tongue ripped out amid crimson gushes of Lewis' patented stage blood. (It was a sheep's tongue, swollen and rotting under the lights and sprayed with Pine Sol.)

Marginally less blood-soaked was the stream of cheap horror films from the Philippines *(The Blood Drinkers, Mad Doctor of Blood Island, Blood Devils, Beast of the Yellow Night, Night of the Cobra Woman.)* Marginally more bizarre was a series of Mexican quickies which pitted local wrestling heroes against various indigenous monsters, the most amusing title being provided by *Wrestling Women vs the Aztec Mummy.*

One exploitation film of the 60s stands out from the mechanistic carnage of its rivals, George Romero's *Night of the Living Dead* (1968). Shot on a shoestring budget in Pennsylvania, it ostensibly chronicles the desperate efforts of a bunch of Middle Americans, trapped in a remote farmhouse, to beat off attacks of an army of walking dead, zombies which have inexplicably risen from the grave or escaped from the morgue. However, plausible arguments have been advanced to place the film in a wider political context: the walking dead are, perhaps, the 'dead weight' of patriarchal authority and the nuclear family, the suffocating traditions on which the order of 'normal' society is based.

Purely as a film maker Romero manages skilfully to undercut the traditions of the horror genre in style worthy of Hitchcock. The apparent heroine lapses into a state of catatonia early in the film; the young couple, society's hope for the future, are burned to a crisp and then return as zombies; the nuclear family who seek shelter in the farmhouse's cellar are eaten by their small daughter. The active, intelligent black hero, with whom the audience automatically sympathizes and who is determined to get everyone to work together, succeeds only in getting everyone killed but himself. At the end of the film he emerges from the farmhouse to be shot by a police posse disposing of the zombies and casually bundled onto a heap of corpses loaded on a pick-up truck. The prelude to his death is punctuated by some marvellously Hitchcockian comic relief as a fat redneck sheriff waddles around giving the audience some useful advice on how to dispose of a zombie with the minimum of fuss.

The subversive influence is also at work in the films of Larry Cohen, an underrated director whose work in the 70s — *It's Alive, It's Alive II, God Told Me To* — presented monsters as the product of the 'normality' which they threaten. Dismissed as run-of-the-mill exploitation fodder, they nevertheless remain disturbing explorations of the ambivalent metaphysics of urban America.

In the 70s the gore extravaganzas moved in from the grind houses and began to invade mainstream cinema. The success of Tobe Hooper's *Texas Chainsaw Massacre* (1974), with its monstrous parody of the Hollywood all-male family tradition, provoked a string of imitators. At the same time the freer sexual climate allowed intelligent directors like Stephanie Rothman to emphasize the sexuality inherent in the vampire legend in *The Velvet Vampire* (1971), which despite its meagre budget is informed with her customary wit and humanity. This contrasts sharply with David Cronenberg's *Shivers* (1975) in which unpleasant little parasites attack the inhabitants of an apartment block, turning them into raving maniacs. Both phallic and scatalogical the parasites reflect an apparently overwhelming disgust with sexuality.

By the end of the 70s sex, violence and horror were combined in a highly successful mainstream cycle of 'knife' movies, in the mould of *Friday the 13th* (1980), in which terrified high school girls are menaced by knife-wielding psychotics, usually one of their number. The most popular heroine of the formula films is pretty Jamie Lee Curtis, a vigorous screamer, the Evelyn Ankers of our own troubled times.

Ian Ogilvy, whose mind is controlled by scientists Boris Karloff and Catherine Lacey, stabs Susan George to death in Michael Reeves' *The Sorcerers* (1967). Reeves' brief but immensely promising career ended with his suicide in 1969. His last film was the minor classic *Witchfinder General*.

Blaxploitation horror. AIP's *Blacula* (1972), which was followed by *Scream, Blacula, Scream*, and an utter farrago which marked AIP's 100th release, *Blackenstein* (1973).

Cinema of the fantastic – Mario Bava's *Planet of the Vampires* (1965).

A long way from Transylvania, John Carradine goes about his grisly work in William Beaudine's *Billy the Kid vs. Dracula* (1966). Beaudine followed this with an even more unlikely combination, *Jesse James Meets Frankenstein's Daughter,* his last film in a career stretching back to 1929.

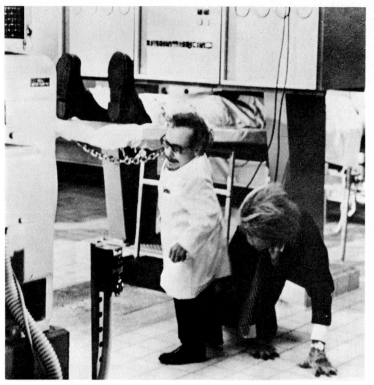

above
I Drink Your Blood (1977)
produced by the appositely
named Jerry Gross. On the
drive-in circuit it is invariably
paired with Del Tenney's *I Eat
Your Skin* (1971).

above left
Dean Stockwell as the
President's press secretary and
part-time werewolf and tiny
Michael Dunn as 'Dr Kiss' (no
relation) in *The White House
Horrors* (1973).

left
Something frightful about to
happen in Tobe Hooper's *Texas
Chainsaw Massacre* (1974).
Made for $200,000, it has
grossed $40 million worldwide.

left
Plus ça change. Harry Lauter (right) and Craig Littler in George Schenk's *Superbeast* (1972), a Philippines-shot quickie which borrows heavily from an old horror classic *The Most Dangerous Game*, originally filmed in 1932 by Ernest B. Schoedsack and Irving Pichel.

below
The monstrous birth in Larry Cohen's *It's Alive* (1972).

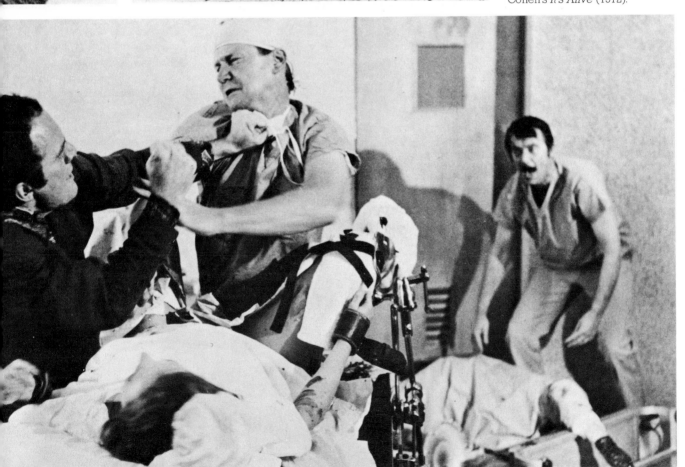

111

DESTROY ALL MONSTERS!
SCIENCE FICTION

'You are not familiar with the focusing disintegrator ray?' blurts the incredulous Derek, the teenager from outer space, in *The Gargan Terror*, Baffled Betty, the pert high school queen confronted with this example of high-tech, can only express mute astonishment. Any afficionado of 50s sf drek would quickly have given her a breakdown of this deadly weapon, fashioned with interplanetary cunning from what appears to be an old hair dryer and wielded by an alien sporting a Bobby Vee haircut and wearing a suit that looks as if it has been hijacked from the wardrobe of *King of the Rocket Men*.

Throughout the 50s the raw material for science fiction cinema lay all around. Get-rich-quick independent producers could lift stories with equal ease from the pages of trash comics or the shrill newspaper headlines which accompanied the Cold War.

At the end of Edward Wood's outrageous *Plan 9 From Outer Space* Criswell the television psychic intones ' . . . someone will touch you on the shoulder and you won't know who it is — they will be from outer space!' At the beginning of the decade a real enough warning for the inhabitants of the plush groves of Bel-Air, although the touch on the shoulder was more likely to be the clammy hand of the House Un-American Activities Committee than that of a Zombie of the Stratosphere. At the same time the American public was bombarded with Cold War newspaper stories chronicling atom tests in the Pacific, the Korean War and the increasingly wild accusation by Senator McCarthy of Communist subversion at the highest levels of government. When reading accounts of the period one cannot go far without stumbling over the word 'paranoia'. It was this climate of hysteria — generated by fear of invasion, atomic war, or the accidental or deliberate misuse of nuclear power — which produced a cycle of classic Bs whose very lack of production values, outlandish plots, incoherent acting and frequently laughable special effects point a demented finger at the deep unease lying beneath the bland surface of Middle America.

The great majority of those movies were made by independent producers, men in a hurry to exploit an expanding market — drive-ins and local cinemas wanting low-rental second or double features — which was not being catered for by the major studios. Their budgets fell pitifully short of those devoted to Jack Arnold's *The Incredible Shrinking Man* or Byron Haskin's *War of the Worlds*. Indeed, they fell as low as the $12,000 Roger Corman lavished on his first feature, *Monster from the Ocean Floor*. Shooting schedules were brisk, to say the least. Edgar Ulmer took eleven

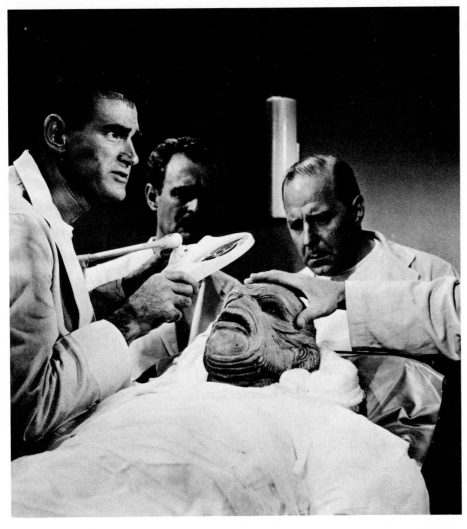

End of a cycle. Jeff Morrow puts Jack Arnold's Gill-Man under the magnifying glass in *The Creature Walks Among Us* (1956).

days to complete *Beyond the Time Barrier* and *The Amazing Transparent Man*, filming them back to back in the unlikely setting of the Texas State Showground. Robert Hutton's *Slime People* was shot in a wholesale meat market in Los Angeles. In *20 Million Miles to Earth*, Nathan Juran ingeniously contrived a dramatic opening — in which a spaceship returning from Venus makes a forced landing at sea — by using sets left over from *Mutiny on the Bounty*. But this seems like *2001* when compared with the special effects in *Plan 9 From Outer Space;* in Edward Wood's epic the flying saucers menacing Earth were nothing more than paper plates. The destruction of the alien spacecraft at the climax of the film was achieved by the simple expedient of soaking one of the plates in gasoline, lighting it and then hurling it towards the camera.

If your space opera began to run out of time, money, sets and ideas, you could always give the plot a neat twist to bring the movie staggering over the finishing line. In *Space Monster* a convenient crash landing in a distant planet's ocean transforms the movie into an underwater actioner, complete with a cut-rate version of the Creature from the Black Lagoon and giant crabs menacing the submerged space ship. This episode contains an unforgettable moment when one of the highly trained crew, gazing thoughtfully at a viewing screen which displays a forest of back-projected claws and eyes on stalks, says with grim scientific conviction, 'I think they must be some kind of crab'.

William Castle learned his trade in the hard school of Monogram. If you could complete a Monogram project on time and within budget, you could make a film for anyone. In his *Project X* (1968), set in the future, the scientist hero is consigned to a simulated version of the past — naturally a location in 60s California — in an attempt to provide the key to a lost secret. Members of the scientific team observing him maintain the illusion by convincing him that he is one of their bank-robbing gang, on the lam after pulling a heist. The need to lie low allows Castle the maximum use of the cheapest possible location, although it puts some strain on the creaking plot. The scientist guardians, moving around uneasily in their 60s clothes, have received only the sketchiest of briefings — the female member has no idea what you do with a potato. Nevertheless our hero, who just happens to be an expert on the history of the 60s, remains too befuddled to penetrate the transparent deception.

Tiny budgets also led to the wholesale plundering of stock footage of natural disasters and scenes of World War II devastation. A particular favourite was the earthquake sequence from Hal Roach's *One Million BC* which turns up at fairly arbitrary moments in such epics as Roger Corman's *Attack of the Crab Monsters* and Phil Tucker's *Robot Monster*. One gets the impression that Al Zimbalist, the producer of *Robot Monster*, would have been quite happy to lash together entire films from stock footage. Sizeable chunks were lifted from *Stanley and Livingstone* for his *Monster from Green Hell*, in which the leads had to wear pith helmets to conceal the deception. The spirited sandbox slugfest between two lizards in *One Million BC* was resurrected by Zimbalist for a 1962 quickie, *Valley of the Dragons*.

Nine years earlier they made one of their many guest appearances in what must be the front runner in the desperation stakes, *Robot Monster*. An alien invader, the Ro-man, has succeeded in wiping out all but six of Earth's population with the deadly Calcinator Death Ray. The discerning viewer will also note that this total victory has been gained with a little help from the Ro-man's friends in the World War II Luftwaffe. The Ro-man was played by George Barrows, a bit-part actor who specialized in ape roles. For *Robot Monster* he wore a moth-eaten gorilla suit with a dented diving helmet jammed on top. His headquarters are located outside a cave in Bronson Canyon, a bleak Hollywood setting used in hundreds of sf cheapies and Western programmers. For an interplanetary conqueror the Ro-man certainly travels light. There is no evidence of his space-ship and his equipment consists of a large mirror with a few knobs attached to the frame, a wooden table on which a number of ancient radio receivers are shakily perched, and a machine which intermittently blows little clouds of bubbles into the wide-open spaces of Bronson Canyon. This final technological marvel is the Automatic Billion Bubble Machine, supplied by N. A. Fisher Chemical Products Inc. For endearing absurdity, the portly Ro-man, flailing his shaggy arms to activate the Calcinator Death Ray, beats off such strong opposition as the monster turkey from outer space in *The Giant Claw*, Gamera the 400-foot turtle, which destroys Tokyo, and Son of Blob. But the price of great art is high. The hoots of derision which greeted *Robot Monster's* release drove its director, Phil Tucker, to a nervous breakdown. To this day, he avers, 'I still do not believe there is a person alive who could have done as well for as little money as I was able to do.'

Someone who might have done better was Roger Corman, throughout the 50s the most prolific producer and director of grade Z trash. The ink on newspaper headlines hardly had time to dry before Corman would move into action. On the day following the launch of the first Russian sputnik, he went to Steven Broidy, president of Allied Artists, and promised him a completed satellite exploitation movie within eight weeks. The result — *War of the Satellites* — is no *2001*, but like the majority of these movies it made money. It also contains a number of the classic elements of 50s sf Bs.

A strange cylinder emanating from Spiral Nebula Gamma warns Earthlings to stay out of space. An energy barrier will be erected round

Insect Invasion

Richard Denning is hauled to
safety in Edward Ludwig's
Black Scorpion (1957).

A giant spider lumbers out of
the Arizona desert in *Tarantula*,
directed by Jack Arnold in 1955.
It was napalmed into oblivion
by jet pilot Clint Eastwood.

A 200-foot long mantis comes to
a sad end in an underground
parking lot in Nathan Juran's
The Deadly Mantis (1957).
Despatched by Craig Stevens'
commando unit, the monster
insect dies magnificently and in
characteristic style, trumpeting
away like a berserk herd of
elephants.

SCIENCE FICTION

Aspects of 50s Unease

left
The biggest syringe in the world in pursuit of *The Amazing Colossal Man* (1957), directed by Bert I. Gordon.

right
Following an encounter with an oversize alien William Hudson's wife (Allison Hayes) has developed a distressing weight problem in Nathan Juran's *Attack of the Fifty Foot Woman* (1958).

below left
Grant Williams well on the way to a rendezvous with infinity in Jack Arnold's *The Incredible Shrinking Man* (1957).

below
Dean Parkin in AIP's *War of the Colossal Beast* (1958).

right
Panic aboard the alien
spacecraft in Edward Wood's
Plan 9 From Outer Space (1959)
as bald zombie Tor Johnson
lunges for extraterrestrial
Dudley Manlove. Tor Johnson, a
sometime wrestler known as
'the Big Swede with a heart of
gold', was a regular fixture in
Wood's movies. Manlove was
the radio voice for Ivory Soap.

Production values were higher
on Universal's *This Island Earth*
(1955), but leaden leads Jeff
Morrow and Faith Domergue
give it that unmistakeable B
patina.

Earth to destroy our manned satellites. The mission of Project Sigma, headed by physicist Dr Van Ponder (Richard Devon), is to blast through the barrier at the speed of light. However, the cards are stacked against the mission as the crafty aliens have replaced the real Van Ponder with an android substitute. Not only can the android clone himself, he also remains unaffected by such minor distractions as a high-powered blow torch being accidentally turned on his hand.

Naturally this raises suspicions in the razor-sharp minds of the crew, particularly Dave Boyer (Dick Miller), whose misgivings increase when he notices that an old scar on Van Ponder's arm is now mirrored exactly by a new one on the other arm. But there's no time to reflect on this as astronaut Sybil (Susan Cabot) hustles Dave into the Sigma rocket — 'It's 45 minutes to blast-off', she cries. Once in orbit, the android Van Ponder starts to run amok. He swiftly manufactures a heart in order to pass a check-up from the mission's doctor and then in a fit of pique murders the hapless medic. However, he gets more than he bargained for with his new organ, as he promptly falls in love with Sybil and is then despatched by a good old-fashioned sock on the jaw from vengeful Dave. It's always reassuring to know that the supertechnologies which produce android supermen or the focusing disintegrator ray have absolutely no answer to a well-aimed right hook straight out of *Holt of the Secret Service*. Dave blasts the satellite through the energy barrier, leaving us with a few well-chosen words in *Star Trek* vein about the new worlds which await us in outer space.

Compared with the almost subliminal production values of *Robot Monster*, *War of the Satellites'* feeble special effects seem positively lavish. But Corman was quite prepared to dispense with them entirely if it was necessary. *The Beast with a Million Eyes* was an economically invisible alien intelligence which forced cattle and domestic animals to turn against their human masters, providing a hint of what was to come seven years later with Hitchcock's *The Birds*. In *Not Of This Earth* the alien menace was provided by Paul Birch in a business suit and a pair of dark glasses. He is a vampire from outer space, sending back blood samples to the irradiated survivors of nuclear war on the planet Dervana. Transfusions of human blood will ensure their survival and eventual conquest of Earth. Calling himself Mr Johnson, the alien rents a ludicrous Beverly Hills mansion, hires a weasel-like petty crook with the unlikely name of Jeremy as a manservant, and pads off at night clutching a briefcase which contains a built-in transfusion kit. Removing his shades to reveal eyes like a pair of ping-pong balls, he proceeds to scramble his victims' brains before draining their bodies of blood. Racing against time Mr Johnson sends a Chinaman back home through a matter transmitter but sadly the Oriental is 'compressed'. Desperate measures are called for. In a hilarious scene Johnson lures a frenzied hoover salesman (Corman regular Dick Miller) down to the basement, where his beady eyes bring an abrupt halt to a torrent of patter about domestic appliances. The drained body is unceremoniously stuffed into the incinerator, only to be swiftly followed by a pathetic gaggle of hoboes, whose blood is likely to give the hapless inhabitants of Dervana rather more to worry about than radiation sickness.

At this point Johnson is paid a visit by girlfriend, who has jumped into the matter transmitter and gone absent without leave. Like Johnson she needs constant transfusions. After nightfall they raid a surgery but in the darkened room Johnson's groping hands alights on a sample of rabid dog's blood which is being stored in the doctor's fridge 'for tests'. 'I feel activity inside me', his companion understandably complains after the transfusion. The death of his companion — and the suffocation of the doctor by means of a bizarre flying parasol released from his briefcase — destroy Johnson's cover. A final desperate attempt to transmit what passes for the movie's heroine back to Dervana is foiled by her dumb cop boyfriend in a wild car

Cold War Frenzy

Morris Ankrum, Peter Graves and Andrea King try to figure out God's wavelength in Harry Horner's bizarre *Red Planet Mars* (1952).

Shielded from the FBI's finest by armoured glass, the mad Nazi/Communist scientist holds America to ransom while, unseen behind him, his grotesque charges close in for the kill in the climax of William Cameron Menzies' *The Whip Hand* (RKO, 1951).

Frankie Avalon, Jean Hagen and Ray Milland have every reason to look a trifle jumpy – Los Angeles has just been flattened by a pre-emptive Russian nuclear attack, in *Panic in the Year Zero*, directed by Milland in 1962.

chase. Ultra-sensitive to loud noises, Johnson is driven off the road to his doom by the scream of a motorcycle klaxon. In the final scene the male and female leads stand over a tombstone which commemorates his grisly end — 'Here lies a man who was not of this earth'. As they move off, the camera pans away to a solitary figure plodding out of the middle distance. He is dressed in a black business suit, wears dark glasses and carries a brief case. Principally because of an impressive performance by the gravel-voiced Birch, the figure of Mr Johnson on his lonely quest, surrounded by a crowd of ugly and crass Americans, assumes a tragic quality which transcends the limitations of a pitifully low budget.

Buried in the plot of *Not Of This Earth* was the reference to the horrific aftermath of nuclear war. The threat of a nuclear holocaust and the dangers attendant on nuclear power — dimly apprehended and barely understood by both the public and B-movie producers — provided themes from which endless variations could be wrung. No matter that a stream of government-sponsored documentaries presented serried ranks of white-coated scientists dispensing reassurances about the dawn of a new era of limitless energy. Everyone knew that it was only matter of time before this breakneck technological helter-skelter produced rampaging hordes of monster insects, 70-foot men and even teenage giants.

A world devastated by nuclear weapons was dealt with in relatively straightforward style in Arch Oboler's *Five* and Alfred E. Green *Invasion USA* (1952), the latter plunging America into an all-out nuclear war with the Soviet Union only to reveal at the end that everything was the result of mass hypnosis. Shot in seven days for $127,000, *Invasion USA* grossed nearly a million. Ten years later in *Panic in the Year Zero*, Ray Milland took to the hills with his familiy, Jean Hagen and teen idol Frankie Avalon, after a Soviet pre-emptive strike flattens Los Angeles. As they flee to the dubious safety of the countryside, repeated shots of the slider on the car radio, moving endlessly back and forth against a relentless background crackle of static, provide a potent image of the breakdown of organized society. Inevitably, Roger Corman provided his own cut-rate version of the end of the world in *The Last Woman on Earth*. In 1964 Vincent Price redressed the balance in *The Last Man on Earth*, a low budget version of Richard Matheson's 'I Am Legend', which many prefer to the subsequent expensive remake, *The Omega Man,* starring Charlton Heston and Anthony Zerbe. In *Battle Beneath the Earth*, the pax Americana is threatened by a renegade Red Chinese general, played in flamboyant Fu Manchu style by Peter Arne, whose high-powered tunnelling machines burrow their way under the Pacific and then the heartland of America, leaving primed nuclear devices beneath major cities and military installations.

Perhaps the strangest example of Cold War hysteria is *Red Planet Mars*, which was released in 1952 at a time when McCarthy's crusade against Communism had reached fever pitch. The screenplay, an incredible hotch potch of moral rearmament clichés onto which is grafted a clodhopping celebration of the virtues of American family life, was written by John L. Balderston whose previous work included the classic *Bride of Frankenstein*. Production designer Charles D. Hall had also worked on this movie, as well as collaborating with Edgar Ulmer on *The Black Cat*. Director Harry Horner was also a designer; fortunately his association with *Red Planet Mars* did not prevent him from subsequently making a distinguished contribution to the academy-award-winning *The Hustler*.

In *Red Planet Mars* a clean-cut young American scientist (Peter Graves) establishes contact with a superior civilization on Mars. The revelation of the Martians' ability to harness cosmic energy has the distressing effect of knocking the bottom out of the West's steel and coal industries, while the news that their life-span extends to 300 years puts an instant chill on the life insurance market. In a montage of newspaper front pages there is a poignant reminder of postwar austerity in Britain as a Fleet Street headline proclaims, 'No Rationing on Mars!'. Further shocks are in store. It seems that the Martians embrace a religion whose resemblance to Christianity is rather less than coincidential. Could God be speaking from Mars? As Earth is gripped by a religious revival, the Communist regime in Russia is overthrown and replaced by a theocracy headed by an elderly bearded Patriarch. The sudden appearance of this Khomeini look-alike adds a bizarre touch to present-day viewing of *Red Planet Mars*. Interestingly, television screenings have often omitted this sequence.

The advent of the millennium is then threatened by the introduction of an Anti-Christ played in manic style by Herbert Berghof. From a remote hideout in the Andes emerges a crazed, drink-sodden scientist (Berghof) — a former Nazi now in the pay of Soviet Russia — who declares that not only is Graves' equipment based on his own wartime experiments but also that he, Berghof, is responsible for all the Martian messages. To save the born-again revival from this shattering disclosure, Graves promptly blows up himself, his wife and Berghof in his laboratory, but not before a final message from God comes over the line — 'Well done, thou good and faithful servants!' A new era of peace and prosperity dawns, with Americans secure in the knowledge that God will vote the Eisenhower Nixon ticket.

The combination of Nazism and Communism is typical of the early 50s. In *Red Planet Mars* the Soviet leaders are portrayed in a style reminiscent of the standard wartime B treatment of Hitler and his henchmen. In William Cameron Menzies' *The Whip Hand* a journalist on a fishing holiday stumbles on a remote mountain resort which has been taken over by a small army of Communist infiltrators in the pay of an ex-Nazi germ warfare expert who disappeared behind the Iron Curtain at the end of the war. He plans to release plague bacilli into America's water supply but at the movie's climax is beaten to a pulp by the grotesque collection of human guinea pigs he keeps in his mountain-top laboratory. He goes down shrieking, 'Communism will rule the world!,'

Cameron Menzies is best remembered for his magnificent production design work on *Gone With the Wind* and his direction of Alexander Korda's *Things to Come*. Towards the end of his career he directed a number of low-budget features, all of which display intermittent flashes of his design genius. His final movie, *Invaders from Mars*, released in 1953, is a genuine curiosity whose principal theme — the possession of individual humans by an alien intelligence — foreshadows such classics of the genre as Don Siegel's *Invasion of the Bodysnatchers* and Gene Fowler Jnr's *I Married a Monster from Outer Space*.

A small boy (Jimmy Hunt) wakes one night to see a flying saucer land in the field behind his home and bury itself beneath a large sandpit. When his genial scientist father (Leif Erickson) goes to investigate, he is sucked down through the sand to the accompaniment of unearthly music. Next morning he is returned, a dishevelled, irrascible automaton with a strange device implanted in the back of his neck. The boy's mother quickly goes the same way, as does little Nancy from next door, two police patrolmen, the chief of police and the local military bigwig General Meybury, who is in charge of the rocket project on which Erickson is working.

Seen from the child's point of view, the transformation of his parents into distant, hard-faced robots is brilliantly handled, particularly a scene in which his glacial mother attempts to take him home from a police station. The use of over-size furniture and a series of strikingly composed shots reflect both the child's confusion and a sense of menace. This is vividly realized in his mother's slow, deliberate advance towards him down the long, bleak corridor which leads from the station's entrance to the duty sergeant's desk.

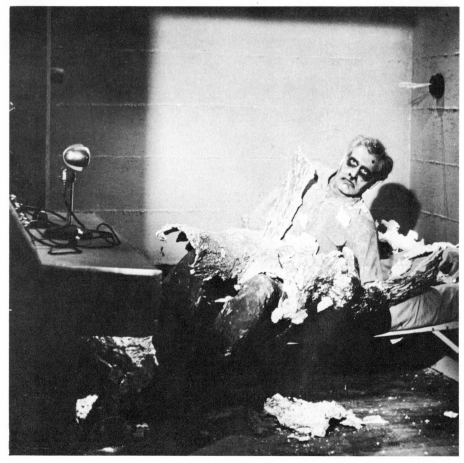

Alien Possession

far left
Little Jimmy Hunt realizes that all is not well with Mom and Pop (Helen Carter and Leif Erickson), and even the local cops are more zomboid than usual in William Cameron Menzies' minor masterpiece *Invaders from Mars* (1953).

left
Kevin McCarthy and Dana Wynter flee from the pod people in Don Siegel's classic *Invasion of the Bodysnatchers* (1956).

far left
This member of the walking dead has been possessed by one of Edward C. Cahn's *Invisible Invaders*, an absurd but inventive 1959 quickie which might have influenced George Romero's *Night of the Living Dead*.

centre
Help me doctor. Returned astronaut Richard Wordsworth slowly turning into a perambulating cactus in Hammer's *Quatermass Experiment*, directed by Val Guest in 1955.

left
It – The Terror from Beyond Space, Edward L. Cahn's 1958 workout for Ridley Scott's *Alien*. The man inside the fright suit is Ray 'Crash' Corrigan, a former hero of the B Western.

Sadly, from this moment *Invaders from Mars* descends into total implausibility. Snatched from his mother by a friendly woman doctor, the boy takes about thirty seconds to convince astronomer Arthur Franz that his story is true. It's hardly surprising as Franz, striding round his observatory, launches into a breathless potted history of everything from unexplained UFO sightings to the 'canals' on Mars. It can only mean one thing — an underground race of Martians are sabotaging the rocket project and planning an invasion. It must be right — after all, Franz is wearing an incredibly hairy tweed coat, and is sucking away furiously at a large pipe.

A few telephone calls and half the US Army are crawling all over the sandpit. A commando unit bursting into the Martians' underground lair find themselves in a complex of tunnels laser-blasted by lumbering green mutants dressed in sagging zip-up boiler suits. The tunnels lead to a controlling intelligence, a strange disembodied head housed in a plastic bubble. Here the sets are strikingly effective, a vision of the future by way of Bauhaus and light years from the tottering banks of obsolete electrical hardware which characterize low-budget science fiction. In an image of haunting beauty the captured heroine is subjected to the operation to implant the mind-controlling crystal into her neck. Her face — passive, unconscious, her forehead resting on her hand — fills the right of the screen in close-up as a sinister needle moves with infinitessimal slowness towards her slender exposed neck.

The stricken Martian saucer bursts through the sandpit, but as it lifts off it is blown apart by delayed-action bombs left behind by the departing troops. As the child flees in terror we see a montage of the traumatic events of the last twenty-four hours superimposed over his running form. The montage whirls us back into his bedroom just as his father closes the door in a sequence which exactly mirrors one at the beginning of the movie. Was it all a dream? A rushing noise draws the boy to the window and once again he witnesses the descent of a flying saucer.

Before its release, *Invaders from Mars* suffered severely at the hands of the studio. The final sequence was cut to preserve the banal and conventional dream ending. The insertion of repeated tank mobilization stock footage becomes most almost obsessive. It also clashes horribly with Cameron Menzies' beautifully contrived studio set of the sandpit which hides the Martian invaders. Heavily foreshortened, with its dramatically colour-streaked sky and elegant, stylized trees, it is a triumph of artifice in the grand tradition of *Gone With the Wind*. *Invaders from Mars* reverberates with these echoes of its director's distinguished past. A fire at the rocket plant recalls the burning of Atlanta. The Martian superbrain, with his shifty eyes and groping tentacles, is a distant relation of the eight-armed automatic assassin of *The Thief of Bagdad*. For many years something of a cult classic, it is heartening to see *Invaders from Mars* now gaining a wider circulation.

The feverish scientific activity of the 50s was bound to alarm extra-terrestrials reluctant to allow earthlings to horn in on what was obviously a fairly crowded market. By now, however, scientists were creating the potential for sufficient havoc on Earth itself to make the lonely efforts of Nyah the Devil Girl from Mars or the Man from Planet X seem relatively puny. Nuclear power fuelled the fantasies of science fiction film makers as powerfully as the triumphs of steam had pumped drama onto the pages of Victorian penny dreadfuls.

The atom-bomb test provided the perfect catalyst. It raised a monster from the deep in *The Beast from 20,000 Fathoms*. Its fall-out nourished a race of monster ants in Gordon Douglas' *Them* and a swarm of giant wasps in *The Monster from Green Hell*. It liberated a violently explosive mineral — element 112 — in Fred Sears' *The Day the World Exploded*. Accidental

far left
I Married a Monster from Outer Space (1958). Despite its exploitation title, director Gene Fowler gave the film a brooding menace which may well have influenced the television series *The Outer Limits,* broadcast in the early 50s.

left
The Monolith Monsters (1957) directed by John Sherwood from a script by Jack Arnold. An alien element, brought to earth by a meteorite, invades human bodies, first turning them to stone and then expanding into gigantic shards of crystal which threaten to engulf the planet.

The cocktail lounge version of the conquest of space.

Cat Women of the Moon, a 1954 cheapie in which rocket men Sonny Tufts and Victor Jory discover an underground female empire on the dark side of the moon.

Zsa Zsa Gabor and her minions have just captured Eric Fleming in the 1958 *Queen of Outer Space.* On this planet, the men have been exiled, but as Zsa Zsa sighs 'vimmen cannot live vizout men'. Watch out Eric.

exposure to atomic blast inevitably produced alarming human mutations: a steel gangster in Allan Dwan's pulsating melodrama, *The Most Dangerous Man Alive;* a 70-foot US Army colonel in Bert I. Gordons *Amazing Colossal Man.*

An AIP quickie, *Amazing Colossal Man* rode in on the coat tails of Jack Arnold's 1957 masterpiece for Universal, *The Incredible Shrinking Man.* An out-and-out exploiter, the movie betrays its minimal budget at every turn, but nevertheless retains a sufficiently lunatic internal logic to catapult it into a realm beyond criticism.

Colossal Man's opening moments provide a memorably raw image of American 'preparedness' during the Cold War. In a slit trench in the Nevada desert Colonel Manning (Glenn Langan) and his men await the night-time detonation of a nuclear device. The screen is filled with tense, helmeted faces in extreme, grainy close-up, their black anti-flash glasses draining them of humanity — perhaps a tiny B echo of the Teutonic knights in *Alexander Nevsky.* As the countdown begins, a light aircraft strays into the area and crashes nearby. Langan races to the pilot's rescue, exposing himself to the full force of the nuclear blast. Rushed to hospital with '95 per cent third degree burns', Langan amazes his doctors by developing a healthy new skin overnight. But every medical breakthrough carries with it the risk of unpleasant side effects, and this is no exception. Langan suddenly starts to grow at the rate of ten feet a day. Moved to an isolated army hospital, he is housed in a circus tent — an ironic reminder of his freakishness — while doctors conduct desperate size-reducing experiments on elephants and camels (perhaps they came in a job lot with the circus tent). Yet another breakthrough, miniature elephants and camels, but will they be in time to save Glenn from cardiac arrest as his undersized heart gives up the unequal struggle to power his oversized body?

By now the distraught colonel has broken out and is stalking about among the back-projected neon signs of Las Vegas. Panic amongst the population seems somewhat less than total, but in this town it would take more than a 70-foot bald giant in a loin cloth to prise the night people away from the tables. Hot on his trail is a scientific team armed with the biggest syringe in the world, filled to overflowing with the shrinking serum. But after a few halfhearted jabs at the giant's ankle, they are forced to watch helplessly as he is shot off the Boulder Dam by a trigger-happy GI with a bazooka.

This untimely end did not prevent Gordon from making a sequel, *War of the Colossal Beast,* with Dean Parkin taking over the role of the unfortunate giant.

Meanwhile, a rival producer was hard at work on one of the all-time schlock masterpieces, *The Attack of the Fifty Foot Woman,* directed by the ubiquitous Nathan Juran. A big tennis ball from outer space disgorges a monster who makes off with poor little rich girl Nancy Archer, heiress to the 'Fowler millions' and owner of the Star of India, 'the most valuable diamond in the world'. Nancy may be a millionairess, but from the look of her living room she spends it all at Woolworths. On her return to the trash palace she gives new meaning to the expression 'being interfered with' by shooting up to a height of fifty feet. Even the dimmest member of the audience will quickly grasp that something is seriously amiss when an enormous plaster of paris hand starts waving at the camera in the master bedroom. Unlike the dithering army doctors in the *Colossal Man,* Nancy's medical advisors make a swift and brutal diagnosis, instantly sending out for chains, meathooks, several gallons of morphine, and an 'elephant syringe'. None of these prevents Nancy from bursting gloriously through the roof of her house and stomping off in search of her wastrel husband Harry. Cornering Harry with his floozy in an all-night beanery, she plucks him delicately from the debris, and holding him aloft like a rather distasteful suppository, crushes him to death. In a fit of anguish she then electrocutes herself on an overhead power line.

Occasionally during this magnificent rubbish the director forgets himself and starts trying to make a movie. There is an effective sequence when the sheriff and his deputy break into the alien spaceship, its floating clouds of gas and distorting mirrors evoking a momentary feeling of unease. Fortunately this is quickly dissipated by the appearance of the alien — an elderly gentleman in a painfully slow-moving and wraith-like process shot who is wearing a dress extra's outfit from *Gypsy Wildcat*.

Fifty Foot Woman also makes repeated use of the *sine qua non* of all rock-bottom sf Bs of the late 50s: a filter shot of a Plymouth Plaza wallowing down a dirt road and carrying a fat sheriff and his idiot deputy towards their rendezvous with destiny.

In a universe where all logic is suspended, anything can happen. In *The Deadly Mantis* a giant insect, roused from its prehistoric slumber by the construction of an Arctic early warning system, descends on Washington from the North Pole; it meets a sad end in that classic no-man's land of American cinema, an underground car park. In *Navy Versus the Night Monsters*, civilization in the shape of Mamie Van Doren is threatened by man-eating plants from the Antarctic; they don't stand a chance. In *Monster on the Campus*, ace pipe-sucker Arthur Franz takes another heavy draw on his briar, impregnated with radio active coelocanth blood, and instantly turns into a homicidal neanderthal man. He gallantly offers himself up to the pistols of the police, but not before scoring a neat bullseye on a forest ranger's forehead with a handy axe. In *Tarantula*, one of the best of the 'giant insect' cycle, Leo G. Carroll's experiments in accelerated tissue growth let a monster spider loose in the Arizona desert. The rampaging arachnid is napalmed in a jet strike led by a young Clint Eastwood.

The combination of scientific mishap, preferably radioactive, and monster insects produced an entire sub-species of movies. Twenty years after his 1957 giant locust epic, *The Beginning of the End*, the indefatigable Bert I. Gordon was producing *Empire of the Ants*, a far-fetched variation of an H. G. Wells short story in which vacationers Robert Lansing and Joan Collins run into an item unlikely to be found in their travel brochure, a tribe of giant ants swollen by a leaking barrel of radioactive waste.

The red-blooded entrepreneur will always strive for the most fanciful combinations, transplanting elements of one genre wholesale into another. A late 50s cross-breeding of hot-rod exploiters, teen pix and alien invasion low-budgeters provided such pulp masterpieces as Edward L. Cahn's *Invasion of the Saucermen*, Tom Graeff's *The Gargan Terror* (a. k. a. *Teenagers from Outer Space*), Del Tenney's *Horror of Party Beach* and Irvin S. Yeaworth's *The Blob*. In the last, Steve McQueen and his hot-rod gang meet blank disbelief when they try to warn the muscle-brained adults that a giant red protoplasm is on the prowl, growing larger with every kill. They soon change their minds when the primeval ooze invades the local cinema.

Sadly, the days are over when carrot men from Venus roamed free among the dusty acres of Bronson Canyon. Society's collapse from within is now sardonically measured in the work of directors like Jeff Lieberman. His *Blue Sunshine* provided the 70s' most chilling epitaph for the flower-children of that bogus *annus mirabilis*, 1967, as the long-delayed effects of a particularly virulent kind of LSD begin to turn middle-class adults into bald, homicidal maniacs.

Yet the spirit of the past can still struggle to the surface. Anyone viewing New World's 1980 *Humanoids from the Deep* will be struck by the monsters' more than passing resemblance to the *Creature from the Black Lagoon*. Forget the fashionable ecology-based plotline. The Gill-man lives!

Unique in cinema is the Japanese Toho studio's cycle of monster epics, the first of which was *Godzilla, King of the Monsters* (1956). In a deliberate attempt to exorcise the horror of the bombing of Hiroshima and Nagasaki, Eiji Tsuburuya's special effects department created a complete monster iconography including Ghidrah, the three-headed dragon *(left)* and Rodan a vast pterodactyl *(below left),* seen here razing Yokohama to the ground. In the fight of the century in 1963 *(top right)* King Kong slugged it out with Godzilla, who seems to be hitting below the belt here. Other monsters included Yog, the giant octopus; Mothra, a huge moth; Matanga, the fungus of terror; and Dogora, a giant jellyfish from outer space. The theme of atomic war and radiation runs through all the films – even in *Frankenstein Conquers the World* (1966) the monster of the title is a human who has grown to colossal size after exposure to radiation. The series climaxed with *Destroy All Monsters* (1968): all the monsters have been imprisoned on an island (a metaphor for nuclear disarmament) before escaping under the control of alien invaders and going on the rampage.

Godzilla's success inevitably produced a host of imitators. On the right are two of them.

The Swedish *Reptilicus* (1962), a marvellous compendium of monster clichés and the British *Gorgo* (1961) in which we find a rather charming male lead taking a paddle in Pool of London with the usual destructive results.

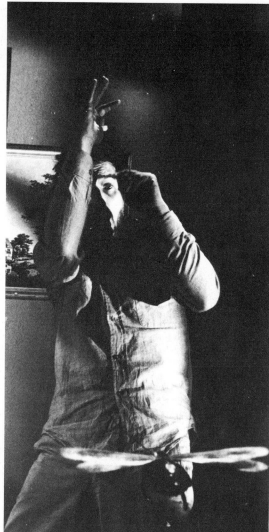

Two William Castle films.

left: Project X (1968)
right: the 1975 *Bug* (produced
by Castle and directed by
Jeannot Szwarc). Crazed
scientist Bradford Dillman is
about to be consumed by a
swarm of giant firebreathing
insects thrown up by a desert
earthquake. This apocalyptic
little movie was one of the best
of the eco-disaster exploitation
cycle of the 70s.

right
As everyone knows, this is what
happens to a housefly when it
alights upon an irradiated
coeclocanth. The effects on
biologist Arthur Franz are no
less alarming in Jack Arnold's
Monster on the Campus (1958).

130

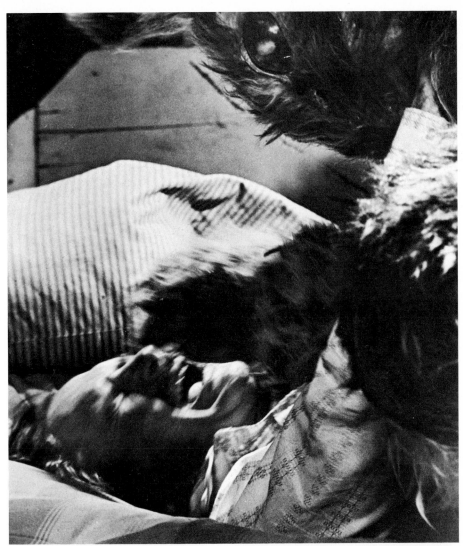

One of the worst films from the eco-cycle, *The Night of the Lepus* (1972), in which an army of 150lb killer rabbits try to take over the Mid-West. Rory Calhoun and Stuart Whitman are on hand to call in the National Guard and save mankind. Throughout the film the giant rabbits remain resolutely unterrifying.

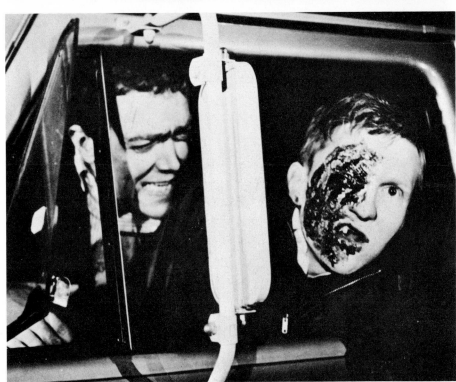

The Horror of Party Beach (1964), in which monsters from the ocean floor try to muscle in on a clam bake with discouraging results.

above
An amoeba from outer space
with an insatiable appetite for
human beings is on the loose
but Steve McQueen seems to
be having difficulty getting the
message across in *The Blob*
(1958). Aspiring star McQueen
received $3,000 for this early
appearance.

You can't keep a good blob
down. Robert Walker is
menaced by an old friend in
Beware! The Blob (1972).
Director Larry Hagman now
plays a Texan blob in *Dallas.*

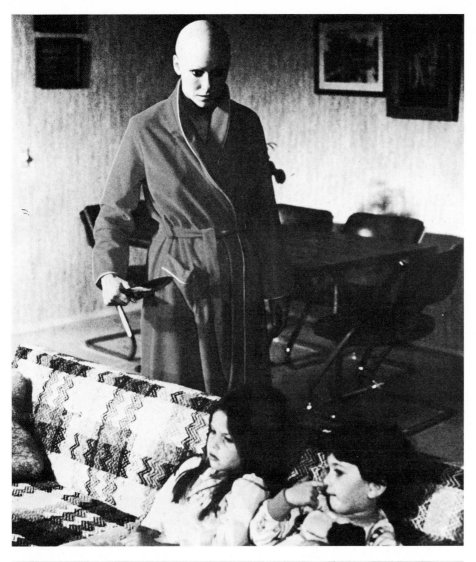

Bad trips in Jeff Lieberman's *Blue Sunshine* (1972), an ironic elegy for former middle-class hippies who, with Haight-Ashbury far behind them, are suddenly turned into bald maniacs, the delayed results of a particularly nasty type of LSD.

Almost the last frame of *Not of This Earth* (1957), but Roger Corman still has a little surprise in store for his audience as yet another on a long line of alien invaders trudges out of the middle distance.

RETREAT, HELL!
B MOVIES AT WAR

During the Second World War the Hollywood dream factory was put on to a war footing. Unlike some American industries, the movie business required a minimum of conversion, effortlessly adapting all the stock genres — crime thrillers, musicals, even the B Western — to accommodate popular war themes.

For the Bs, always prone to rely on stereotypes and to underline rather than question popular preconceptions, the result was a stream of low-budget actioners whose shrill patriotism and cut-rate heroics must have seemed embarrassing to audiences even at the time. At the beginning of the American involvement there was something appropriate in the tub-thumping patriotism of George B. Seitz's *A Yank on the Burma Road*, in which New York taxi driver Barry Nelson leads a caravan of medical supplies over the Burma Road to China. However, as the conflict dragged on few people remained unacquainted with the realities of war, and this inevitably undercut the juvenile antics of films like Mongram's *Wings Over the Pacific* (1943) in which Edward Norris kills Nazi spies, overwhelms a Japanese landing party and wins the hand of Inez Cooper before handing over an island to the US Army as a enemy-free base. In Gordon Douglas' *First Yank in Tokyo* (RKO, 1945) B veteran Tom Neal undergoes plastic surgery in order to be smuggled into Japan in a bid to free a captured weapons expert. Two years earlier, in Edward Dmytryk's *Behind the Rising Sun,* Neal had played a Japanese-American persuaded by his father (J. Carrol Naish) to participate in the Japanese invasion of the Chinese mainland in the 1930s, only to be disgusted by their barbaric methods of waging war.

For harassed wartime film makers the perennial problems posed by low-budgets and ten-day schedules were compounded by price limits on set construction, the rationing of blanks and film stock and an increasing manpower shortage. The draft hit everyone from leading men to technicians; at Fox, for example, the studio had to make do without B leading men Jeffrey Lynn, Craig Stevens, Ronald Reagan and Wayne Morris. (Even producers of horror films were deprived of a better-class of zombie extra, as John Carradine discovered in Steve Sekely's 1943 *Revenge of the Zombies* in which he sets about building a zombie army for the Führer in the swamps of Louisiana.) The result was often 'jaw, jaw, not war, war', a failing by no means confined to Bs of the 40s. In Monte Hellman's Philippines-shot quickie *Back Door to Hell* (1965), the substitute for action is Jack Nicholson throwing out lines like 'Your'e the kind of guy who'd call Mahatma Gandhi a rabble rouser!' In Roger Corman's inventive

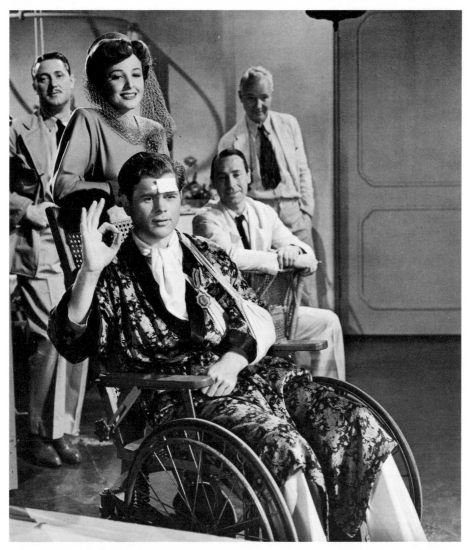

Bloody but unbowed. Laraine
Day and Barry Nelson in
George B. Seitz's *A Yank on the
Burma Road* (1942), the first film
to celebrate America's entry
into the war.

Noel Madison, Anna May Wong
and Leslie Denison at the top of
the steps in Joseph H. Lewis'
stylish PRC second feature
Bombs Over Burma (1942).

135

Secret Invasion (1964) — whose plot foreshadows *The Dirty Dozen* — the cracks begin to show when the action starts, despite a small army of Yugoslavian extras. Jack Starrett's *The Losers* (1970) — a Joe Solomon exploitation movie — suffered as much from implausibility as a low budget. Originally titled *Nam's Angels,* it dealt with a suicide mission in Cambodia undertaken by a unit composed of Hell's Angels.

One result of the wartime stringencies was a spate of submarine movies. For cast-conscious producers their attraction lay in the extended use of one set, the sub's interior, and the studio's miniature tank. However, like the exploits of their land-based colleagues, the submariners' adventures stuck fast in a Sargasso Sea of high melodrama. The first of this sub-genre was Columbia's 1942 *Submarine Raiders* in which John Howard fails to warn Pearl Harbor in time of the imminent Japanese attack and has to settle for a duel with a lone enemy aircraft carrier which has Marguerite Chapman held prisoner on board. Subsequent submarine epics were cast in the same mould: they included *Out of the Depths* (1943) with Jim Bannon, *Two-Man Submarine* (1944) with Tom Neal and *U-Boat Prisoner* (1944) with Bruce Bennett. The last two were directed by the tireless Lew Landers.

Far more interesting were the B movie's attempts to come to grips with Nazi psychology. An early straw in the wind was *The Beasts of Berlin,* released in 1939 by PRC after a great deal of dithering, and dealing with underground resistance to the Nazi regime. It was an unremarkable little film but it did have Alan Ladd in a small part. Ladd's rocketing wartime popularity ensured a speedy re-release and a new title, *Hell's Devils,* with the new star's name at the head of the cast list. The same fate overtook Phil Rosen's *Paper Bullets,* a 1941 PRC gangster B with Ladd in a supporting role.

Inevitably, B exposés of Nazi Germany opted for sensationalism at the expense of accuracy, although hindsight has sadly bestowed on them a retrospective justification. Much was made of Nazi eugenic theories. In Steve Sekely's *Women in Bondage* (1943), shortsighted Nancy Kelly is deemed unfit to marry her SS sweetheart. Her subsequent anti-Nazi outbursts condemn her to an enforced sterilization. Similar themes were explored by Edward Dmytryk in *Hitler's Children* (1943), in which Tim Holt and Bonita Granville undergo the ruthless indoctrination aimed at German youth. In MGM's *Hitler's Madman,* directed by Douglas Sirk, John Carradine hammed it up as Reinhard Heydrich, Nazi governor of Czechoslovakia and perpetrator of the Lidice massacre. As the *New York Times* remarked, 'Here in one diatribe MGM's assortment of authors have summoned up practically every indictment against the Nazis that they could crowd into one film.' A similar approach was adopted in the 1944 *Enemy of Women* in which Paul Andor played Dr Josef Goebbels, Hitler's Minister of Propaganda. Herbert J. Biberman's *The Master Race* (1944) provided a more intelligent attempt to analyse the dynamics of Nazism. George Coulouris gave a fine performance as an SS Colonel posing as a Belgian patriot and plotting an uprising against the American occupation forces. This was a far more honest examination of the horrors of occupation and the mixed blessings of liberation than resistance melodramas like *The Black Parachute* (1944) with Larry Parks, *The Night Is Ending* (1944) with George Sanders, and *Chetniks, the Fighting Guerillas* (1945) in which Dutchman Philip Dorn (a war refugee himself) played the Yugoslav resistance leader General Mihailovic, a man who was about to become the plaything of history.

Even these films seem like masterpieces of realism when compared with far-fetched efforts like Alfred E. Green's *Appointment in Berlin* (1943), in which smooth George Sanders was a 'Lord Haw Haw' type working inside Germany for British Intelligence. Unfortunately he was unable to link up with the Invisible Man, Jon Hall, who was parachuted into Berlin in 1942 to thwart Nazi Sir Cedric Hardwicke's plans to invade America. During this period back-lot Berlins were seething with spies of the unlikeliest kind. In RKO's 1943 *Passport to Destiny*, charlady Elsa Lanchester goes to Germany to kill Hitler. Nick Grinde's 1943 PRC quickie *Hitler, Dead or Alive* set a comic band of conmen off on a bid to kidnap Hitler for a reward. The Führer was played by Bobby Watson, who was kept busy impersonating the demon king in films as disparate as the broad comedies *The Devil With Hitler* (1942) and *The Nazty Nuisance* (1943) and John Farrow's melodramatic attempt to explain the Nazi phenomenon in *The Hitler Gang* (1944).

While Nazi Germany was being undermined by Mrs Mops, flim-flam men, Invisible Men and improbable double agents, it seemed that every American war plant was menaced by saboteurs. The Bs dealt with this mainly imagined threat in a way that left little to the imagination in action-packed second features like *They Came to Blow Up America* (1942), which set double agents George Sanders and Anna Sten against FBI man Ward Bond, and *Stand By All Networks* (1942) in which John Beal played an ace radio reporter on the trail of enemy agents. In these films it was an easy matter for scriptwriters to substitute Nazi spy rings for the racketeers exposed by the daring newshounds' pre-war colleagues. In *Spy Ship*, for example, directed in 1942 by Western stalwart B. Reeves Eason, reporter Craig Stevens steps in to rescue lovely Irene Manning from the clutches of a band of traitors/mobsters.

Frequently these brisk little actioners were given a heavy shot of morale-boosting regeneration. In *I Escaped From the Gestapo* (1943) forger Dean Jagger is forced to work for an Axis spy ring, decides to go straight and helps the FBI to bring them to book. Tom Neal plays a racketeer drafted into the Army in D. Ross Lederman's *The Racket Man* (1944). He turns over a new leaf, uncovers a black market gang and then makes the supreme sacrifice. The same fate awaited peacetime deserter Richard Arlen in Paramount's 1943 *Minesweeper*, he rejoins the Navy, falls in love with Jean Parker and sacrifices his life in order to gain the secrets of a new mine.

The boosting of morale and the encouragement of recruiting and war service were aims readily adopted by the Bs. Even a slim little PRC musical like *Harvest Melody* (1944) was given a serious 'Help the Farmers' theme, as was Edgar Ulmer's *Jive Junction* (1943). The benefits of rigorous training were chronicled in Warners' 1943 *Three Sons O' Guns*, in which a band of ne'er do wells make good in Uncle Sam's Army. In *There's Something About a Soldier* (1943), Tom Neal and Bruce Bennett make their way through Officers' Training School with romantic interest provided by Evelyn Keyes. Paramount's *The Navy Way* (1943) showed how the usual cross-section of raw recruits reacted to basic training. John H. Auer's *Gangway for Tomorrow* (1943) concentrated on war industry, telling the stories of five different factory workers: a French refugee (Margo), a racing driver (Robert Ryan), a prison warder (James Bell), a beauty queen (Amelita Ward) and a hobo (John Carradine). Auer also directed the 1940 *Women in War*, an early attempt by Republic to depict life in wartime Britain, with Wendy Barrie and Mae Clark playing two volunteer nurses who fall for handsome Patric Knowles. Republic was always quick to exploit events on the other side of the Atlantic; *The London Blackout Murders* (1942) had John Abbot, of the sinister, staring eyes, systematically disposing of the inevitable Nazi spy cell.

The humorous side of service life was celebrated in a host of slapstick comedies which seldom rose above the level set by Wally Brown and Alan Carney, a kind of low-budget Abbot and Costello, who starred in a number

above
Japanese-American Tom Neal is beginning to regret having volunteered for the Sino-Japanese conflict as he tries to persuade his senior officer Beal Wong not to give opium to the conquered Chinese in Edward Dmytryk's *Behind the Rising Sun* (1943).

left
Secret agent Larry Parks under the desk in Lew Landers' *The Black Parachute* (1944). Jonathan Hale is king of an occupied Balkan country and Ivan Tressault is the Nazi officer.

below
George Sanders and Marguerite Chapman at a border crossing – a minor masterpiece of studio artifice – in Alfred E. Green's 1943 *Appointment in Berlin*.

of wartime Bs for RKO, including *Adventures of a Rookie* and *Rookies in Burma*. Probably the most embarrassing comedy effort was Monogram's mercifully shortlived attempt to launch a Private 'Stuffy' Smith series starring Bud Duncan; if for nothing else, it will be remembered for the marvellously titled *Hillbilly Blitzkrieg* (1943).

The war also gave the B series a shot in to the arm. Sherlock Holmes, The East Side Kids and The Lone Wolf entered the list with *Sherlock Holmes and the Secret Weapon* (1942), *Junior Army* (1943) and *Passport to Suez* (1944). Even Lassie became an Army dog in *Courage of Lassie* (1946). The Sherlock Holmes adventures invariably ended with a sub-Churchillian harangue from Basil Rathbone on the 'Why We Fight' lines, with Nigel Bruce mumbling agreement in the background. More rooted in wartime reality were pointed little comedies like *Johnny Doesn't Live Here Any More* (1944), which dealt with the cramped living conditions resulting from the war effort, and *Weekend Pass* (1944), directed by Jean Yarbrough, in which shipyard worker Noah Beery Jnr earns a bonus and a weekend with pay and then meets runaway Martha O'Driscoll.

The problems that might face returning soldiers provided the theme of Steve Sekely's *My Buddy* (1944), which starred Don Barry, Ruth Terry and Lynne Roberts. Told in B flashback style, the film begins with priest John Litel telling the Postwar Planning Committee in Washington of the sad tale of Eddie Ballinger (Don Barry) who returns home a hero from the First World War only to drift into unemployment and then gangsterism (something of a lift from the 1939 James Cagney vehicle *The Roaring Twenties*). The film concludes with a stirring plea from Litel that the Committee ensures that veterans from the present conflict do not meet the same fate.

The Korean War gave veteran directors like Lew Landers and Lesley Selander a chance to churn out production-line Cold War action Bs which differed little from their Second World War predecessors. In *A Yank in Korea* (1951), *Battle Zone* (1952), and later efforts like *War Is Hell* (1964) grim-faced Marines repel the faceless Commie hordes from the safety of studio-bound trenches. Lewis Seiler's *Bamboo Prison* (1954) provided a *Master Race* in reverse, with Robert Francis posing as an informer in a North Korean prisoner of war camp. Even films in the hands of intelligent directors, like Joseph H. Lewis' *Retreat, Hell!* (1952), are stocked with familiar types like grizzled Colonel Frank Lovejoy bellowing, 'Your'e a Marine and don't you forget it', to wobbling reserve officer Richard Carlson. Despite the time-honoured montages of training camp and library footage of the Inchon landings, the skilful Lewis manages to extract a glimmer of anti-war sentiment from the predictable storyline. In this he is helped by a sympathetic performance from Russ Tamblyn as a frightened youngster trying to live up to his family's Marine traditions. One tightly orchestrated sequence in which Tamblyn wins his spurs by knocking out a machine-gun nest remains in the mind.

The best low-budget Korean film, and certainly one of the best of the post-1945 war films, was Sam Fuller's *The Steel Helmet.* Shot in ten days on a budget of $104,000, it develops as a crash course in battlefield survival; the central character, a battle-hardened, cynical sergeant (Gene Evans) guiding a tyro lieutenant's lost patrol to an artillery observation post located in a Buddhist temple.

The themes set out in *The Steel Helmet* — particularly that of the endless recycling of material in combat, with the dead providing handy supply stores for the living — were re-explored at greater length and expense in Fuller's *The Big Red One* (1980). Nevertheless Fuller's earlier film retains a jagged power, right from its opening shot when a seemingly abandoned helmet, against which the credits have rolled, slowly rises to reveal Gene Evans suspicious, watchful eyes, the eyes of a man determined to survive.

left
Macdonald Carey and Marta
Torren have just captured a
German submarine which
refused to surrender after the
war. After a quick wash and
brush up, they try to figure a
way of signalling this information
to surface vessels in *Mystery
Submarine* (1950) directed by
Douglas Sirk.

Bathtime for Hitler. Bobby
Watson as the Führer in *The
Devil with Hitler* (1942).

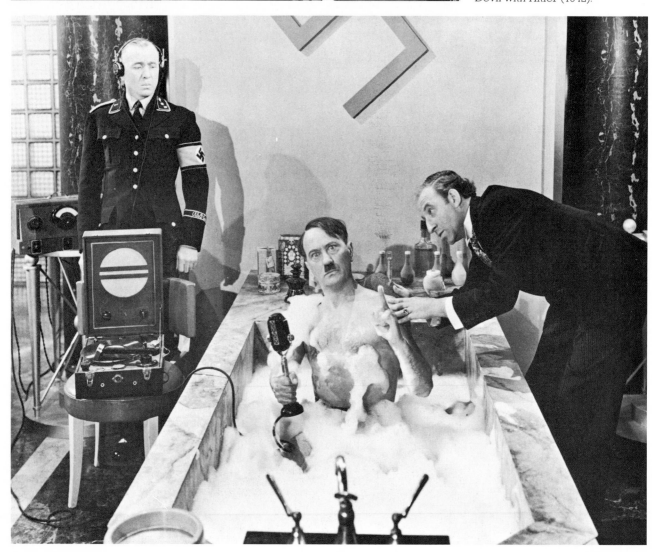

Moral uplift. Jane Frazee entertains in *Rosie the Riveter* (1944).

below
Columbia's *There's Something About a Soldier* directed by Alfred E. Green in 1943, one of a host of wartime recruiting stories. Robert Stanford is the fourth from the left in the first line; John Hubbard is sternly clutching the flag and Bruce Bennett is on the far right.

The Bs effortlessly absorbed the war into all the established film genres.

left
MGM's *Dangerous Partners* (1945), directed by Edward L. Cahn, was a glossy thriller with a Nazi spy ring plot. Signe Hasso and James Craig – seen here receiving a spot of medical attention – played a couple of shady characters who in a sudden rush of patriotism help to break up Edmund Gwenn's spy ring.

right
Nigel Bruce and Basil Rathbone consider the saboteur problem in *Sherlock Holmes and the Secret Weapon,* directed by Roy William Neill in 1942.

right
Tom Drake, Lassie and Elizabeth Taylor in Fred Wilcox's *Courage of Lassie* (1946) in which the canine lead becomes a wartime killer dog before settling back into civilian life.

left
Press censorship. Ace reporter John Beal is dragged from the 'phone by a gang of saboteurs in Lew Landers' 1942 *Stand By All Networks.*

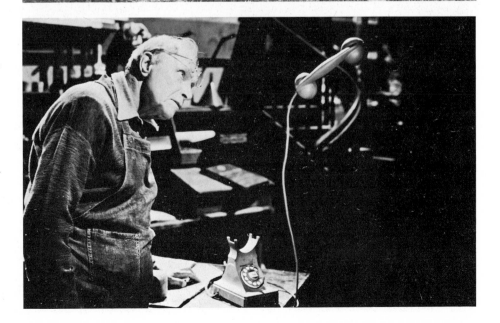

right
Even Invisible Man Jon Hall became a spy in *The Invisible Agent* (1942).

The B movie attempts to come to grips with Nazi psychology.

opposite
Nancy Kelly is manhandled by the SS to the sterlization unit in Steve Sekely's *Women in Bondage* (1943).

left
John Carradine, as Reinhard Heydrich, threatens Lidice's schoolmaster Tully Marshall in Douglas Sirk's *Hitler's Madman* (1942).

left
Tim Holt in Edward Dmytryk's *Hitler's Children* (1943), based on George Ziemen's book 'Education for Death'.

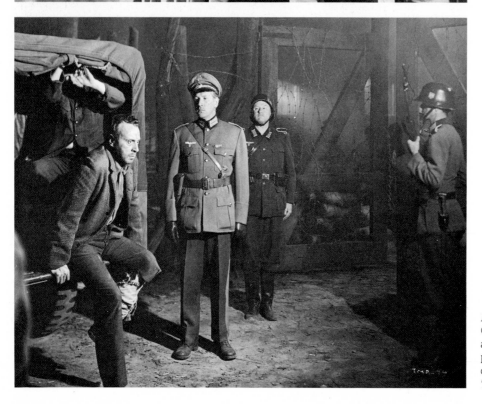

left
George Coulouris, a German agent posing as a Belgian patriot, arrives at a concentration camp in Herbert J. Biberman's *The Master Race* (1944).

right
RKO's *The Brighton Strangler*
(1945) directed by Max
Nosseck. John Loder played an
actor driven mad by an air raid
injury who starts to live out his
stage role, 'the Brighton
Strangler'. The idea was
recycled as an A in George
Cukor's *A Double Life* (1947)
with Ronald Coleman.

Down-to-earth comedy in Willis Goldbeck's *Rationing*. Storekeeper Wallace Beery is about to become the father-in-law of Dorothy Morris, daughter of Marjorie Main, his next-door-neighbour and ration board supervisor.

Elsie and Doris Waters, the much-loved British comedy duo Gert and Daisy, seek shelter in London's underground during the Blitz in *Gert and Daisy's Weekend* (1941).

Simone Simon (left) and James Ellison in *Johnny Doesn't Live Here Any More* (1944), a precursor of *The Apartment*, with crowded wartime conditions making Simone's apartment busier than Grand Central Station.

Second front now. Excitable
Russian army officer Eve Arden
in wartime Washington in
Doughgirls (1944). Jane Wyman
has her fingers in her ears, Ann
Sheridan and Alexis Smith keep
their cool.

Readjusting to civilian life puts a
strain on Lee Bowman and his
wife Jean Arthur in *The
Impatient Years* (1944).

The Andrews Sisters in *Private
Buckaroo* (1942), an army camp
show, one of dozens of Universal
musicals with wartime settings.

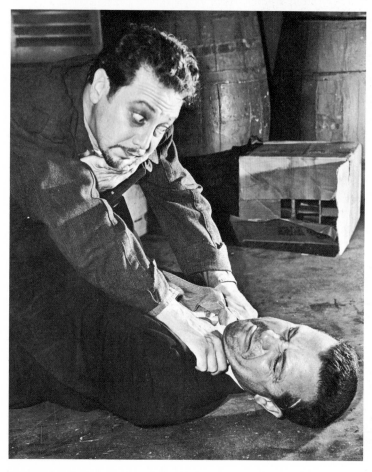

148

At times during the Cold War it seemed that only Frank Lovejoy stood between the Commies and democracy.

far left
He grits his teeth in *I Was a Communist for the FBI* (1951).

left
Joseph H. Lewis' *Retreat, Hell!* (1952) found him face to face with the Reds in Korea.

above
The men who fight and the women who wait. Linda Christian and John Hodiak in Lesley Selander's 1952 *Battle Zone*.

left
Richard Loo and Steve Brodie in the foreground in Samuel Fuller's *The Steel Helmet* (1951).

below
It would be unforgiveable to conclude this chapter without a Foreign Legion picture, so here are George Raft and Marie Windsor swapping brittle conversation over the biggest bowl of couscous in Fez in Robert Florey's *Outpost in Morocco* (1949).

far left
The legacy of war. Luther Adler and Dick Powell at each other's throats in *Cornered*, directed by Edward Dmytryk in 1945. Powell played a Canadian Air Force ace who travels through Europe and South America to track down the Nazi killers of his French wife.

left
The only good Jap . . . Walter Sande gets tough with the enemy in Ray Enright's *Gung-Ho!* (1943), a mind-boggling exercise in blaring jingoism.

149

SWINGIN' ON A RAINBOW
MUSICALS
AND COMEDIES

'We looked like the Ritz brothers in drag', one of the Andrews Sisters remarked of the thirteen musicals they made for Universal during the wartime years. When thinking of the Bs it is all too easy to be dismissive of the dozens of low-budget musicals and comedies turned out at the end of the 30s and into the mid-40s. As Andrew Sarris wrote, 'Nothing is more depressing about a bad movie than its bad jokes or its failed musical numbers or its unimaginative slapstick.' This sour judgement echoes critics of the time. When the Andrews vehicle *Give Out Sisters* was released in 1942, the *New York Herald Tribune* complained, 'In spite of the priority on rubber, Universal Pictures stretches a short subject into a feature-length film by the simple expedient of combining several variety acts with a slight and ineffective plot.'

There was no denying the skimpy, low-budget look of Monogram musicals like *Melody Parade*, starring Eddie Quillan and Mary Beth Hughes, *Sweethearts of the USA* with Una Merkel and its big production number 'You Can't Brush off a Russian', or Arthur Dreifuss' *Sarong Girl*, spotlighting burlesque queen Anne Corio. Sam Katzman's attempts to provide knockabout comedy at Monogram resulted in dreadful efforts like *Three of a Kind,* with Billy Gilbert and Maxie Rosenbloom, which even 'poverty row' must have found embarrassing. Who now remembers Jinx Falkenburg musicals like *The Gay Senorita* or *She Has What It Takes?*

Rarely reviewed, and if they were, frequently in scathing terms, these modest little films nevertheless provided a temporary escape for audiences who wanted to forget the drudgery of war effort production lines and their anxiety for the boys overseas. A giant like MGM may have held itself aloof from the B musical, but Universal plunged in, between 1938 and 1945 producing nearly 100 musical 'entertainments'. The qualification is necessary as many of these Universal second features were films with music rather than full-blown musicals. On a maximum ten-day shooting schedule and with a $50,000 budget, any attempt to provide the Busby Berkeley touch was doomed to failure. After their success in 1938 with *Freshman Year*, starring William Lundigan and Constance Moore, Universal began to turn out a dozen musical comedies a year. They were crammed to bursting point with musical numbers, frequently indigestible slabs of roughhouse comedy and the inevitable romantic subplot. The demands of the production line could, on occasion, lead to regrettable short cuts. When comedian Harold Lloyd saw Universal's 1944 *Her Lucky Night,* he realized that much of the comic business had been lifted straight from his own films. This was hardly surprising as the film's script had been

Constance Moore puckers up
for Dennis O'Keefe in the
complicated love tangle *I'm
Nobody's Sweetheart Now*
(1940) directed by Arthur Lubin.

written by Clyde Bruckman, who had directed Lloyd's *Movie Crazy* in
1932. Lloyd successfully sued Universal for plagiarism.

Universal frequently built their musicals around a current hit song, a
good example being *I'm Nobody's Sweetheart Now* (1940), with Constance
Moore in fine vocal form as a nightclub singer stuck on Dennis O'Keefe.
Directed by the experienced Arthur Lubin, it makes light work of a
complicated romantic tangle between Moore, O'Keefe, Helen Parrish and
college boy O'Keefe's footballing rival, burly Lewis Howard. O'Keefe's
relaxed and amiable comedy style enlivened many Universal second
features in the 40s as he skilfully negotiated his way through the pratfalls of
minor films like *Good Morning, Judge* (1943). Here he plays a music
publisher torn between his grumpy singer girlfriend Mary Beth Hughes
and pert lawyer Louise Allbritton, who is suing him for plagiarism (shades
of Harold Lloyd). Allbritton looks marvellous in severe suits and neckties;

Hughes takes a break from harassing O'Keefe to warble a song which instantly evokes the era, 'Spellbound/Darling, with you I'm wedding bell bound'. In *Good Morning, Judge*, the wedding bells ring for Allbritton, a talented actress who rarely got the chance to move out of the B range to which she was confined by bigger Universal stars like Rosalind Russell. Typical of her output was *That Night With You* (1942), in which she plays a waitress with Broadway ambitions trying to convince impressario Franchot Tone that she is his daughter. In Reginald LeBorg's *San Diego, I Love You* (1944) she's inventor Edward Everett Horton's daughter, single-handedly trying to keep a madcap family together and sell father's latest brainwave, a collapsible life raft. The unpretentious little film achieved a mild success. *Newsweek* commented, 'With every right to expect the worst from a title like *San Diego, I Love You*, the chronic moviegoer may be in for a pleasant surprise. Turning to war-crowded San Diego, Universal has frothed up a little farce that turns methodically zany at every whipstich, but somehow manages an air of spontaneity.' This spontaneity was carried through to a charming scene in which Allbritton persuades bus driver Buster Keaton to kick over the traces and take a moonlight drive along the beach.

B musicals were full of second-string versions of bigger stars. The British ice-skating champion and actress Belita got the Sonja Henie treatment in Republic's *Ice Capades* (1941) and *Lady Let's Dance* (1944). At Universal Gloria Jean had to make her way in the shadow of Deanna Durbin in films like *Pardon My Rythym* and *Reckless Age* (both 1944). After the success of the 1942 *What's Cooking?* she partnered Donald O'Connor in a number of youth-angled frolics (among them *Get Hep to Love* and *It Comes Up Love*) which earned them the tag of an ersatz Mickey Rooney-Judy Garland pairing. The Ritz Brothers had to play third fiddle at Universal to Abbott and Costello and Olsen and Johnson, although this did not prevent them from contributing pleasant little comedies like *Behind the Eight Ball* (1942), directed by W. C. Fields veteran Edward F. Cline. In the following year, in *Never a Dull Moment*, the slapstick trio had the support of an excellent B cast, Frances Langford, Mary Beth Hughes, fussy Franklin Pangborn and George Zucco, taking a break from more familiar 'mad doctor' roles. In 1944, Universal's queen of the Bs Evelyn Ankers took time off from being menaced by Lon Chaney Jnr to make *You're A Lucky Fellow, Mr Smith*, a production-line romantic comedy with music in which she marries soldier Allan Jones in order to satisfy the conditions of a will and then realizes, when about to be divorced, that she really loves him.

Another star of the Bs was Jane Frazee, bringing charm and talent to routine projects like Lew Lander's *Swing in the Saddle* (1945) for Columbia and *Swingin' on a Rainbow* for Republic in the same year. In the latter she plays a songwriter who comes to New York to seek justice from a bandleader who has stolen her songs (plagiarism strikes again). She stays to find romance with struggling lyric writer Brad Taylor. The silent comedian Harry Langdon also appears in a fleeting cameo. The director was the versatile William Beaudine, who seemed equally at home in cut-rate actioners, shockers, or musical comedy.

The swing motif runs through many musicals of the period. In Edgar Ulmer's PRC quickie *Jive Junction* (1943), swinging young musician Dickie Moore captures the heart of classically-oriented Tina Thayer. It was not one of Ulmer's happiest efforts; he told Peter Bogdanovich, 'I wanted classical music against jive and you couldn't do it for the money I had. And, of course, it was propaganda to get the kids in America working on the farms during the war.'

In Columbia's 1945 *Hit the Hay*, milk-maid Judy Canova rather improbably goes into the opera business and then astounds the audience by 'swinging it'. Early in the 40s Canova had become the equally unlikely queen of Republic's musical Bs, starring in creaky but enjoyable vehicles

Ann Miller made a number of lovely musical Bs for Columbia during the Second World War.

In *What's Buzzin', Cousin?* (1943), Jeff Donnell, Carol Hughes and Leslie Brooks (extreme left) watch while Ann Miller dances to the music of Freddie Martin and his orchestra.

Victor Moore's appearance causes something of a stir with Ann Miller, Jeff Donnell and members of Kay Kyser's band in *Carolina Blues* (1944).

A production number B style from *Reveille with Beverly*, Columbia's most successful B of 1943, which cost a mere $40,000.

Republic were specialists in Westerns and serials but the studio could turn its hands to musicals.

far left
Judy Canova in Joseph Santley's *Sis Hopkins* (1941), which gave her a chance to mix her own cornball variety of humour with excerpts from 'La Traviata' and tunes by Jule Styne and Frank Loesser.

left
Guest star Roy Rogers well wrapped up in another Republic ice spectacular, *Lake Placid Serenade* (1944), with the film's star Vera Hruba Ralston.

bottom left
Dorothy Lewis in *Ice-Capades* (1941), which also featured Vera Hruba Ralston and Belita with comedy relief from Jerry Colonna and Barbara Allen.

top right
Johnny Coy and a bevy of vivacious showgirls in *Hats off to Rhythm*.

right
Youth on Parade, a typical Ruth Terry vehicle.

Buster Keaton, Jon Hall and Louise Allbritton in Reginald LeBorg's charming Universal comedy *San Diego, I Love You* (1944).

above
Behind the Eight Ball, a 1942 Ritz Brothers romp directed by W. C. Fields veteran Edward F. Cline. Al, Jimmy and Harry watch as Dick Foran is hustled away on suspicion of murder. As it's wartime the culprit turns out to be a Nazi agent masquerading as a member of the Sonny Dunham band.

top right
The Andrews Sisters in Universal's *Her Lucky Night* (1944). Its screenwriter Clyde Bruckman's plagiarism of some Harold Lloyd routines led to a lawsuit which ruined Bruckman's career.

Strange goings on in the tropics.

above
Tahiti Nights, a Jinx Falkenburg musical for Columbia in 1943.

right
Sam Stark and Reed Hadley come to the rescue of Eddie Bracken in Paramount's 1943 *Rainbow Island* directed by Ralph Murphy.

like Joseph Santley's 1941 *Sis Hopkins*. In this adaptation of an old Mabel Normand silent hit, country bumpkin Canova goes to stay with her sophisticated young city cousin Susan Hayward. Canova manages to squeeze some new tunes by Jule Styne and Frank Loesser in amongst the slapstick. Two years later Styne combined with Sammy Cahn to provide two memorable numbers for Republic's *Youth on Parade* with Ruth Terry, 'I've Heard That Song Before' and 'You're So Good To Me', proving that the Bs were not inevitably dustbins for second-rate material.

One first-rate star on the Columbia lot in the early 40s was Ann Miller. The leggy hoofer made a number of lively Bs for the studio during the war years, among them *What's Buzzin' Cousin?* (1943), *Eve Knew Her Apples* (1945) — a rehash of *It Happened One Night* — and *Eadie Was a Lady* (1946). In the last, directed by Arthur Dreifuss, Miller plays a college girl who leads a double life as a burlesque queen. The wartime *Reveille With Beverly* (1943), directed by the dependable Charles Barton, repaid its modest $40,000 outlay many times over. Ann Miller played a young disc jockey on an early morning radio programme (hence the title). In a clever device she introduced each musical act by putting on a record, the labels growing larger as the disc spun round to reveal the guest stars. They were a distinguished bunch, including Bob Crosby, Freddie Slack, Count Basie and Duke Ellington with their respective orchestras, the Mills Brothers, the Radio Rogues, and a very young Frank Sinatra. Sinatra gave a svelte rendition of 'Night and Day' in a cut-price version of a Busby Berkeley routine surrounded by a budget bevy of attractive pianists and violinists. An impressed critic wrote, 'I'm convinced there has been nothing like him since goldfish eating'. The later Sinatra craze was exploited in Glenn Tryon's *Meet Miss Bobby Sox* (1945), an enterprising Columbia B with Lynn Merrick and Louise Erickson.

That fine comedian Leon Errol wrested a laugh from Sinatra's emaciated good looks in Universal's *She Gets Her Man* (1945). Playing an arthritic cop on a murder hunt in a small-town theatre, he bumps into a prop skeleton; 'Oh, another crooner', he mutters absentmindedly. In *She Gets Her Man*, Errol was teamed with comedienne Joan Davis, a vaudeville veteran who could wring laughs from the most palsied script. The theatre setting provided Davis with the raw material for some fairly basic slapstick. During the performance of a jungle drama, 'Voodoo Princess', she inadvertently switches on the rain and snow effects, deluging the hapless actors. Later, she wanders around with an unseen balloon stuck to her jacket and gently tapping her head; as she repeatedly swerves around in panic, the balloon drifts out of her eyesight. In true B fashion, at the end of the film the assassin is revealed in peremptory style — 'Murder was his hobby', is Davis' simple explanation.

In 1944 Joan Davis was teamed with Jane Frazee in two Columbia Bs, *Kansas City Kitty* and *Beautiful But Broke*. In the latter, along with Judy Clark, they form an all-girl orchestra to exploit the wartime shortage of male musicians. Stranded in the middle of nowhere, the girls unwittingly seek shelter in a hut in the middle of an army test firing range. Their sleep is rudely interrupted by a barrage of shells whose blast conveniently deposits them all in the branches of a nearby tree!

The 40s were the golden age of radio, and a number of attempts, most of them unsuccessful, were made to promote radio stars in the cinema. In *Radio Stars on Parade*, the humour was provided by Wally Brown and Alan Carney. *How Do You Do?* was a modest comedy featuring Bert Gordon, the radio comedian known as the Mad Russian. *I'll Tell the World* was a fast-talking comedy with a radio background starring Lee Tracy. *Take It or Leave It* was a novelty film based on a famous American radio programme, as was *National Barn Dance*, a reminder of the days of pre-television innocence.

above
A plump young Yvonne de Carlo with Maxie Rosenbloom and Byron Foulger in Columbia's embarrassingly unfunny *Harvard Here I Come* (1942) directed by Lew Landers.

top left
Judy Canova and Joe E. Brown down on the Dude Ranch in Joseph Santley's 1943 *Chatterbox*.

left
Laurel and Hardy in *Nothing But Trouble* (1944), directed by Sam Taylor.

Vince Edwards, Jack Carson and Bert Lahr in *Mister Universe*, a 1951 spoof of the wrestling business directed by Joseph Lerner.

Comedy Monogram style –
*Jiggs and Maggie in Jackpot
Jitters* (1949), directed by
William Beaudine.

Allyn Joslyn seems amused by
the playful mood of police
woman Carole Landis' dog in *It
Shouldn't Happen to a Dog*
(1946) directed by Herbert I.
Leeds.

Frankie Lane in *Rainbow
'Round my Shoulder* directed in
1952 by Richard Quine. Ah, for
Ann Miller.

159

WHY, SIR JASPER, CAN I FIX YOU A DRINK?
EPICS AND COSTUME DRAMAS

Many years ago I sat watching a late-night movie, a cut-rate swashbuckler whose title now eludes me. In her bedroom, a bizarre Hollywood stab at a genuine eighteenth-century ambience (salvaged perhaps from a more lavish production), the heroine — no doubt Faith Domergue, Jean Wallace or Patricia Medina — goes about her toilet. Suddenly at her window appears Sir Jasper or Sir Roger, or perhaps Sir Gawain — take your pick from George Montgomery, Cornel Wilde or Louis Hayward — seeking shelter from his enemies, the chief of which was almost certainly either George Macready, Berry Kroeger or John Sutton. But our heroine is equal to the situation; it's at least the third time that Sir Jasper has chosen this unconventional method of dropping in for a chat. Confronting him, she trills, 'Why, Sir Jasper, can I fix you a drink?'

Such sublime anachronisms litter B costume melodramas. Vincent Price, as Omar Khayam in *Son of Sinbad* (1955) muses during a brief period of incarceration, 'To sleep, perchance to dream. That's a thought worth embroidering. But at the moment I'm too busy — I'll leave it to another poet.' In the same film the corpulent Caliph of Baghdad (Leon Askin) lisps to the slave girls, 'Back to the harem, and don't wait up for me!' Bluff Crusader David Farrar had a useful line in medieval small talk in the 1954 *Golden Horde,* rapping out to a Middle Eastern princess, 'In my country they burn lunatics at the stake. You should try it some time.' In the *Bandit of Sherwood Forest* (1946) Cornel Wilde is provided with an opening line more appropriate to Central Park than the leafy glades of Lincolnshire — 'What's a pretty girl like you doing in Sherwood Forest?'

The unspoken answer to this question might well have been, 'fulfilling my Universal contract.' During the late 40s and the early 50s Universal and Columbia produced a steady stream of cost-conscious costume melodramas and Technicolor mini-epics, low-budget versions of escapist spectaculars like MGM's *Adventures of Quentin Durward* and Fox's *Prince of Foxes,* which were filmed abroad, in England and Italy respectively, using up credits frozen by European governments after the Second World War.

Many of these movies were directed by veteran Western hands (Lew Landers, George Sherman, Ray Nazarro and Lesley Selander) who could be relied on not to allow the dialogue to get in the way of the action. Waiting for them on the set were assorted Western character actors — Lloyd Corrigan, Edgar Buchanan, Harry Cording and Ray Teal — who were pressed into service as Merrie Men, Guy of Gisborne's henchmen, pirates and Arabian Nights brigands, not always with the happiest of results. Chain

The yardstick by which any cut-rate costumer must be measured. Exotic Maria Montez arouses her subjects to unspeakable evil when she dances the cobra kootch in Universal's 1944 *Cobra Woman*, directed by Robert Siodmak.

mail and Lincoln green could not conceal a style more appropriate to the latest Charles Starrett or Whip Wilson oater.

The 76-minute cousins of the lavish Tyrone Power and Robert Taylor vehicles gave the studios a chance to put second-rank leading men, like George Montgomery and Ricardo Montalban, and promising younger leads, like John Derek and Robert Stack, into tights and through a few brisk athletic paces. It gave the stars a chance to bare their manly torsos, usually as they were strapped to the rack by a bald, leather-clad heavy with George Macready snarling away in the background in a silk dressing gown. Producers calculated that male cinemagoers paid to see the ritualized leaps from balconies onto waiting horses, rapier duels up and down the battlements of Universal's medieval castle, and Patricia Medina's heaving bosom. Studio publicists were convinced that the female members of the audience had other things on their minds. A Columbia handout gleefully announced, 'Girls enjoy watching the hero's rugged torso . . . and many an uninhibited young lady has written to Columbia Pictures asking for a photograph of John Derek in *Rogues of Sherwood Forest* wearing skintight pants.'

On occasion these films shared more than directors and heavies with the B Western. Whether set in medieval Baghdad or nineteenth-century Italy, plots developed along lines that would have been quite familiar to inhabitants of the Bar 20 Ranch. A recurring theme brings the hero back from the Crusades (Civil War) only to confront him with the death of his father at the hands of a grasping croney of King John (railway/cattle baron). Thus does *The Saracen Blade* (1954) present Ricardo Montalban with the same mission of vengeance as the 1936 *King of the Pecos* gave John Wayne.

Amid all the jousting, bone-gnawing and gypsy carousing there were also mandatory interruptions for stirring declarations of faith in a version of constitutional monarchy which, in the Middle Ages at least, would have

left
Cornel Wilde draws a bead in George Sherman's 1946 *Bandit of Sherwood Forest*. On the left, by way of Dodge City, are Ray Teal as Little John and Edgar Buchanan as Friar Tuck.

right
Dashing John Derek is a prisoner of Diana Lynn and Lowell Gilmore in *Rogues of Sherwood Forest* (1950) directed by Gordon Douglas.

left
Six years after *Diary of a Chambermaid* Paulette Goddard's career was on the slide. Here she is with Richard Ney in Edgar Ulmer's *Babes in Bagdad* – a Danzigers' production of 1952.

far left
Rock Hudson thrashes away in Bagdad to win the fair hand of Piper Laurie in Nathan Juran's *The Golden Blade* (1953).

right
Dale Robertson sweet-talking Mari Blanchard in *Son of Sinbad* (1955) directed by Ted Tatzleff.

guaranteed a one-way ticket to David Farrar's stake. In *Rogues of Sherwood Forest* — one of the 'son of Robin Hood' cycle — John Derek, assembled barons and the Archbishop of Canterbury swear to uphold 'The God-given rights of life, freedom and human dignity', before Derek kidnaps King John and forces him to sign the Magna Carta. Our heroes may be outlaws, but subversives they are not. Their aim is the defence or restoration of legitimate authority as embodied in the monarch. Even bad King John — most maligned and misunderstood of British monarchs — is allowed to remain on the throne; after all he is the King. Ultimately the monarchy is seen as the repository of a benign, disinterested authority, under constant threat from the machinations of power-crazed Ministers (Berry Kroeger in *Sword of Monte Cristo*) or Grand Viziers (George Macready in *The Golden Blade*). The monarch himself is not necessarily portrayed in a flattering light. In *Sword of Monte Cristo*, set in the France of the 1850s, the Emperor Napoleon III is a dandified vacillator, more interested in playing billiards and puffing away at new-fangled cigarettes than in the antics of his scheming Minister, Laroche, and it is left to Paula Corday and George Montgomery to come to the defence of the throne.

Sword of Monte Cristo exploits two recurring themes — the masked avenger and the female swashbuckler — combined here in the person of Paula Corday, by day the lady Christianne, by night the Masked Cavalier. In Edgar Ulmer's 1946 PRC quickie *Wife of Monte Cristo*, Lenore Aubert doubled up as the Masked Avenger and the Countess of Monte Cristo. Such an 'entertainment' was a long way from bleak little films noir like *Detour* and *Ruthless,* but Ulmer was nothing if not versatile. His *Pirates of Capri,* shot in Italy in 1949 on a very low budget, is boldly choreographed and full of stirring action, with Louis Hayward playing the effete, foppish Count of Amalfi, in reality Captain Sirocco, the masked champion of freedom battling an evil Police Minister (Rudolph Serato). Ulmer packs the film with stylish versions of all the genre clichés — headlong pursuits up endless flights of steps, furious moonlight rides through the sleeping countryside, and battles at sea. The film opens with the capture of an arms ship by the pirates of Capri while a troupe of actors and tumblers in Commedia Dell'Arte costumes perform on deck. *Pirates of Capri* is full of witty playful references to Ulmer's sophisticated theatrical background in Weimar Germany. The Count of Amalfi is a theatrical dilettante and the final duel with the villainous Holstein takes place on the stage of the court theatre. When I met one of the producers of *Pirates of Capri* he expressed surprise at the intense critical attention lavished on Ulmer in recent years. Although reluctant to agree that Ulmer had anything more than a modest talent, he did add that the director 'talked a great game'.

No amount of talking, expert scripting by skilful writers like Jack Pollfexen and Aubrey Wisberg (who were particularly adept at wringing endless variations from the work of Alexandre Dumas *père*), or cleverly staged fights by Fred Cavens and Ralph Faulkener, could disguise the low budgets on these films. Like the B Westerns, the constant use of stock footage and standing sets bred an easy familiarity with the audience. In 1954 Tony Curtis wielded mace and shield in the Universal castle in Rudolph Maté's *Black Shield of Falworth*. Twelve months later his rapier flashed against the same background in H. Bruce Humberstone's *The Purple Mask*, set in Napoleonic France. *The Black Arrow Strikes,* a Crusader 'revenge' melodrama with Louis Hayward, made use of sets left over from Joseph H. Lewis' 'A' feature, *The Swordsman,* and costumes from *Bandit of Sherwood Forest*. *Sons of the Musketeers,* released in 1952 with Cornel Wilde and Maureen O'Hara, borrowed the sets from William Dieterle's *Hunchback of Nôtre Dame*. The genesis of Frederick de Cordova's *Yankee Buccaneer* reveals the speed with which these films could be improvised. In 1952 the filming of *Against All Flags*, a medium-budget pirate adventure starring Errol Flynn, was interrupted when the sagging film idol broke his ankle. While Flynn recovered, the sets were altered, another script written and another film shot — *Yankee Buccaneer* with Jeff Chandler. Fifteen years later the recycling continued apace. A feeble 1967 remake of *Against All Flags* — *King's Pirate*, with Doug Mclure in the Flynn role — lifted all the big action sequences from the original.

In addition to being frequently saddled with the wooden presence of Paul Henreid, cheap pirate movies relied heavily on set pieces from more lavish productions. Felix Feist's *Pirates of Tripoli* revived the sea battle from *The Golden Hawk*. Sidney Salkow's 1954 *Prince of Pirates* — a piece of hokum about the Dutch Sea Beggars — resorted to large chunks of the 1948 *Joan of Arc*. Robert D. Webb's *Pirates of Tortuga*, one of the waning cycle of British pirate adventures of the 1960s, used several miles of footage from Henry King's 1942 *Black Swan* with Tyrone Power.

Similar films, like *Devil Ship Pirates* and *The Scarlet Blade*, were scraping the bottom of the barrel, but the life had long since gone out of the swashbuckler. Television had delivered the final blow several years before. By the mid-50s American television audiences were being treated to a wide range of imported 30-minute British adventure series: *The Adventures of Robin Hood* with Richard Greene; *William Tell* with Conrad Phillips; *Ivanhoe* with Roger Moore. Despite their miserly bouts of studio-bound action, they helped to drive their low-budget cinema predecessors off the screen. In Hollywood Biblical spectaculars were now all the rage, and waiting round the corner were the natural successors to all those Paul Henreid cloak and rapier adventures — the spear and sandal epics of the Italian musclemen.

'Do you like gladiator movies, son?' asks the closet queen pilot in *Airplane*, summoning up a vanished late-50s world of beefcake, locker room bravado and 'working out' with the boys. A world crammed with slabs of cartilage like corrugated cardboard and Charles Atlas pulling trains along with his teeth. In this sweaty universe, a special niche was reserved for the well-oiled upper torsos of movie musclemen Steve Reeves, Gordon Scott, Reg Park, Kirk Morris and Mark Forrest. Their glistening pectorals and bulging biceps rippled through a series of adventures in which Muscle Beach met Alma Tadema in a delirious cocktail lounge version of the classical world. This phalanx of strongmen provided the exact male equivalent of that great fetish of the day, the startling C-cup charms of perennial B starlet Mamie Van Doren.

The Steve Reeves spectaculars were the logical result of the Italian cinema's long love affair with lavish historical dramas. Their immediate predecessor was the 1949 *Fabiola*, starring Michèle Morgan, Henri Vidal and Michel Simon, a generously budgeted epic in which the Roman aristocracy plan to massacre the Christian population as Constantine marches on Rome. But *Fabiola* was only one of a long line of films stretching back through Fascist propaganda like *Scipio Africanus* to the pioneering pre-1914 work of Enrico Guazzoni *(Quo Vadis?, Brutus, Agrippina)* and Giovanni Pastrone *(Cabiria, Maciste in the Lion's Den)*. The Maciste character, a legendary strongman, was created for *Cabiria* by the Futurist poet and aviator Gabriele D'Annunzio, and his immediate success with the public resulted in a number of sequels starring a burly docker, Bartolomeo Pagano. The durable Maciste was still flexing his muscles in the early 60s. In 1961 five Maciste films were produced in addition to three Hercules adventures and the debut of another strongman hero, Ursus.

A former Mr Universe, Steve Reeves had been appearing in Italian spectaculars since the 1954 *Athena*. However, it was as the eponymous hero of the 1957 *Hercules* that he hit the jackpot. Joseph E. Levine's

The Clinch

above
Yvonne de Carlo and Richard
Greene in Universal's 'romance
of the passionate East', *The
Desert Hawk* (1950), directed
by Frederick de Cordova.

right
Jacques Serenas and Belinda
Lee in *Nights of Lucretia Borgia*
(1959). A former Rank starlet,
the talented Lee's career
declined to cardboard Italian
swashbucklers. She died in a
car crash in 1961.

Suzan Ball, Jeff Chandler and Scott Brady in *Yankee Buccaneer* (1952), a Universal pirate quickie hurriedly thrown together by the studio while Errol Flynn recovered from a broken ankle incurred while filming *Against All Flags*.

Roddy McDowall, Sue England and Dan O'Herlihy in Monogram's modest 1948 *Kidnapped* directed by William Beaudine.

Maria Montez accepts the offer of a twirl around the ballroom floor with Rod Cameron while Gale Sondergaard and Philip Reed look on in *Pirates of Monterey* directed by Alfred Werker in 1946.

Embassy company snapped up the distribution rights for a mere $100,000, and the veteran showman launched a huge publicity campaign which succeeded at the American box office to the tune of at least $5 million. Levine's methods are legendary. For the follow-up, *Hercules Unchained*, he threw a monster thrash in Hollywood complete with a giant ice statue of Reeves fitted with coloured bulbs for muscles. The 700 guests and assorted hacks each took away a 4lb statuette of the now world-famous strongman. In Britain, Levine spent the unheard of sum of £60,000 on publicity, complete with a 50-foot float touring south-east England and a massive television advertising campaign leading up to the nationwide release of the film in the summer of 1960.

The floodgates were opened. In 1957 Italian studios produced only ten costume dramas. Three years later, in 1960, they were working overtime to produce 37, and the next four years saw the production of over 150 European-financed adventures set in the ancient world. Until the advent of the spaghetti Western, they provided the staple of the Italian film industry, and cinema with a new word, *peplum*, coined by French critics who thought highly of the new genre.

Riccardo Freda, director of *Giants of Thessaly* and *Samson and the Seven Miracles of the World*, chose to give a rather portentous gloss on the *peplum*. 'What I am interested in is, roughly speaking, the hero: mankind in times of greatness, in times of war. History is full of possibilities for enthralling scenarios. The main thing is to hit upon the decisive moments.' However, for such an experienced director of exploitation material, the 'decisive moment' was the international market's apparently insatiable appetite for muscleman epics rather than any turning point in classical history.

Any passing authenticity in the *pepla* was purely accidental. Admittedly Sophocles and Aeschylus might have recognized playfully transplanted elements of their work in *Hercules Unchained*, but the dialogue falls some way short of their high standards. The minimal acting ability of the *pepla's* interchangeable leading men, intoning their dubbed lines with all the feeling of a garage full of speak-your-weight machines, led to some hilarious attempts to recreate the conversation of the heroic age. 'You croak like a bird of ill omen', warns Steve Reeves in *Duel of the Titans*, a loosely based version of the tale of Romulus and Remus. In *Ulysses Against the Son of Hercules*, an irate Ulysses exclaims, 'He who eats alone, chokes alone.' Difficult, perhaps, to follow such a copper-bottomed conversation stopper, but the gluttonous Emperor Vitellius might have managed a come-back. In *The Terror of Rome Against the Son of Hercules*, he vouchsafes us this observation: 'I like food best of all in the world. I wish I had the neck of a giraffe and the stomach of an elephant, so I could enjoy it even more.'

The predictable, and reassuring, absurdities of dialogue combined with formula plots to produce the effect of a gigantic comic strip, reminiscent of the *fumetti* — photo stories with balloons — so popular in the Italian magazines. There are frequent interruptions for trials of the hero's strength: the discus is hurled over the horizon; passing stuffed lions and rubber crocodiles are ruthlessly mangled; grunting bald wrestlers are tossed about like so many cabers at the Highland Games, polelaxing job lots of pursuing soldiery in the process; and there are regular bursts of manacle whirling after Hercules-Goliath-Ursus-Maciste has broken free from his prison bonds.

This limbering-up activity is often watched by an evil queen (Sylvia Lopez in *Hercules Unchained*, Fay Spain in *Hercules Conquers Atlantis*) who has the hots for the hero but is not above slipping him a Micky Finn in his Samian wine, or manoeuvering him over a convenient trap door in the floor of the temple. There are aristocratic turncoats with distinctly Fascist tendencies. In *The Giant of Marathon*, the beastly cad Theocritus goes over to the Persian invaders, does not hesitate to plant a spear in the back of his girlfriend and then ties the lovely Mylene Demongeot to the ram on the front of his war galley. If the setting is Roman, as in *The Last Days of Pompeii*, it's likely that decadent aristocrats are trying to pin the blame for a series of murders (executed by their own assassins) on the Christian community. In these circumstances the hero finds himself involved with a small underground group, sometimes of gladiators (*The Secret Seven* is a straight lift from *The Magnificent Seven*, with gladiators instead of gunmen) battling against tyranny. There is much talk of freedom and equality, usually delivered by a right-hand man with only slightly less impressive pectorals than Steve Reeves — Mimmo Palmora played dozens of these roles — climaxing in a revolt of the masses. The tyrants are toppled from the battlements or disappear under an avalanche of bouncing polystyrene masonry.

In order to increase the international appeal of the *pepla*, if not their coherence, a motley collection of well-known American names were recruited. Broderick Crawford played a Greek version of Huey Long in *Goliath and the Dragon*; Bob Mathias, the Olympic decathlon champion, flexed his muscles in *Warlord of Crete*; Jayne Mansfield and her consort Micky Hargitay starred in *The Loves of Hercules*; Rory Calhoun, more at home in stetson and chaps than a toga, proved to be a relaxed and witty leading man in *The Colossus of Rhodes.*

The Colossus of Rhodes was directed by Sergio Leone, and his bold use of space and the film's sudden eruptions of sadism foreshadow the scheme of *A Fistful of Dollars*. Much of the film is dominated by the Colossus itself, straddling the harbour entrance and filled with complex, creaking machinery which pours boiling oil on the ships beneath. In one memorable sequence, Rory Calhoun emerges from the monster's ear to fight several soldiers on its horizontal upper arm. The centre of the screen is dominated by the brutal sightless face, heedless of the tiny figures hacking away at each other beneath.

The fantastic elements in these scenarios gave inventive technicians like Leone and the cinematographer (and later director) Mario Bava a chance to experiment and indulge themselves. *Giant of Marathon* was nominally directed by Hollywood veteran Jacques Tourneur, but much of the credit for its lush, swooning colours and exotic imagery must go to Bava. A long and surrealistic underwater battle beneath the invading Persian war fleet bears his unmistakable mark. It is in such sequences that the directors of the *pepla*, deprived of large Hollywood budgets, achieve on a small scale a mixture of sadism and often startling sensuality which is the hallmark of the best of the genre.

Inevitably, in a number of films all ties with the classical world were severed. Hercules found himself pitted against Gengis Khan in *Hercules Against the Mongols* (1960); against the Incas in *Hercules Against the Sons of the Sun* (1963); against Spanish pirates in *Hercules and the Black Pirate* (1962); battling with werewolves in *Hercules, Prisoner of Evil* (1964); and, finally, adrift in the Big Apple in *Hercules in New York* (1970), a sad end to a cycle which at its height offered — and occasionally delivered — spectacle at its most exotic. What red-blooded male of the early 60s could resist the exhortations of the poster advertising *Warlord of Crete*; 'SEE the captive maidens sacrified to the minotaur monster — half-man, half-beast! SEE the fabled palace of King Minos! SEE the goddess of the sea rise from the depths to claim her mortal lover! SEE the raging revolt of the Cretans! SEE the dread labyrinth of the storied golden thread! SEE the yawning pit of terror where dogs howl for victims! SEE man and monster battle to the death! SEE the ritual dance before the jaws of the awesome idol!' Phew, beat that!

At sword's point.

right
Louis Hayward in Edgar Ulmer's stylish *Pirates of Capri* (1949).

below
Out of the shadows came the masked avenger – Lenore Aubert in another Ulmer costumer, *The Wife of Monte Christo* (1946).

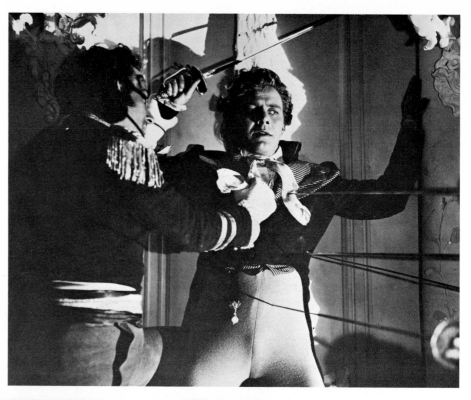

right
Steve Reeves seems to be having some trouble with his chariot in *Hercules* (1959).

Muscleman epics are invariably suffused with a campy eroticism which is perfectly captured here.

right
A tearful Sylva Koscina investigates Steve Reeves' bulging thighs in *Hercules Unchained* (1960).

far right
Similar antics in a surreal landscape in *Hercules, Samson and Ulysses* (1965).

above
Steve Reeves displays
characteristically tasteful
shoulder wounds in *Hercules
Unchained.* A certain amount of
stylized sadism was skilfully
administered in these films by
directors like Riccardo Freda,
Pietro Francisci and Vittorio
Cottafavi.

top right
Kirk Morris uses his formidable
brain power to hypnotize a boa
constrictor in *The Witches'
Curse* (1961), a Maciste
adventure directed by Riccardo
Freda.

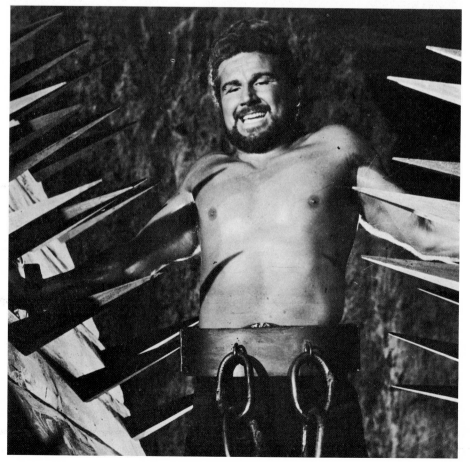

right
Steve Reeves was by far the
most clearly defined Hercules,
but he had a legion of rivals.
Here Alan Steel is put to the test
in *Hercules Against the Moon
Men* (1964).

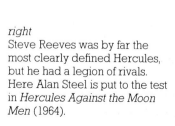

Another Maciste – Mark Forrest – going for a quick submission in *Maciste the Mighty* (1960).

When not chain whirling or lion mangling, the muscleman was often prey to the wiles of an evil priestess or queen. Fay Spain, wicked ruler of the lost city of Atlantis, swarms all over a reluctant Hercules, this time Reg Park, in *Hercules Conquers Atlantis* (1963) directed by Vittorio Cottafavi.

173

Steve Reeves is about to settle with the dastardly Sergio Fantoni while Mylene Demongeot tries desperately to keep her balance in the climax of *The Giant of Marathon* nominally directed by Jacques Tourneur but with a substantial contribution from Mario Bava.

Rory Calhoun contrives to look elegant in what must have been a rather uncomfortable outfit in Sergio Leone's *Colossus of Rhodes* (1961).

right
Victor Mature has his man down
during hand-to-hand combat in
Edgar Ulmer's cut-rate biopic
Hannibal (1959). The helmets of
the attentive soldiery have
obviously seen service in many
another classic epic.

below left
Anne Heywood is about to
provide a succulent propitiary
offering to the Phoenician god
Moloch in *Carthage in Flames*
(1959).

below right
A last chance to admire those
rippling pectorals. Steve
Reeves is proclaimed victor
ludorum in *The Giant of
Marathon.*

WHY CAN'T YOU LEAVE HIM ALONE?

TEEN TORMENT

The problems of 'youth running wild', of teen agony and guilt-ridden parents did not spring ready-made in the mid-50s from the 'teeming gumbo' of Sam Katzman's semiconscious. No doubt the great entrepreneur, who claimed to have invented the word 'beatnik', would have protested loudly at the suggestion, but the distant origins of the 50s teenpix cycle can be traced back to the early 30s. In the 50s a combination of economic and social factors turned what had been a small, underground stream, trickling away in the lower depths of Hollywood's exploitation strata, into a brief, spectacular torrent.

Distraught Fay Wray may well have wrung her hands in despair over her dragster son's antics in AIP's 1958 *Dragstrip Riot*. An impulsive lad, to be sure, but with his heart in the right place. Her worries, however, pale in comparison with those of an earlier generation, victims of the 'guilty parents' syndrome, on which peg was hung many an exploiter of the 30s and 40s. These films were nothing if not consistent. Failure to impart the facts of life was inevitably visited with the direst of consequences. In the 1934 *Guilty Parents*, Jean Lacey, ignorant of those vital facts, runs off with her boyfriend, helps him hold up a gas station, has an illegitimate baby, goes on the booze and finishes up in a seedy burlesque chorus line. The 1935 *Road to Ruin* and *High School Girl* both hammered home the message that parental neglect leads straight to a rude awakening in the maternity ward of a charity hospital. The road to hell is always paved with the best of intentions. In *Secrets of a Model* (1940), one of nine films directed that year by the tireless Sam Newfield, country girl Rita Wilson arrives in the big city hoping to become a model in order to support her invalid mother. Instead she falls into the oily clutches of Jack Thorndyke, and goes through sheer hell before rescue arrives in the shape of gormless milkman Bob Gray.

A far worse fate lay in store for the innocent marijuana smoker. In *Tell Your Children* (a.k.a. *Reefer Madness*, 1939), a high school kid finds himself accused of a murder committed by a crazed reefer fiend. Ten years later a celebrated drugs bust gave Sam Newfield (this time using his 'Sherman Scott' alias) a chance to churn out a minor classic of the genre, *Wild Weed*.

In 1949 Bob Mitchum experienced a little local difficulty, undergoing a brief period of imprisonment on a narcotics possession charge. One of the girls embroiled in this affair was a bit-part actress called Lila Leeds. After her release from prison she starred in a rock-bottom quickie rushed out in the summer of '49. She plays a chorus girl who takes one puff on a stick of tea and becomes instantly hooked. The resulting degradation drives her studious college boy brother to suicide. Throwing herself on the mercy of

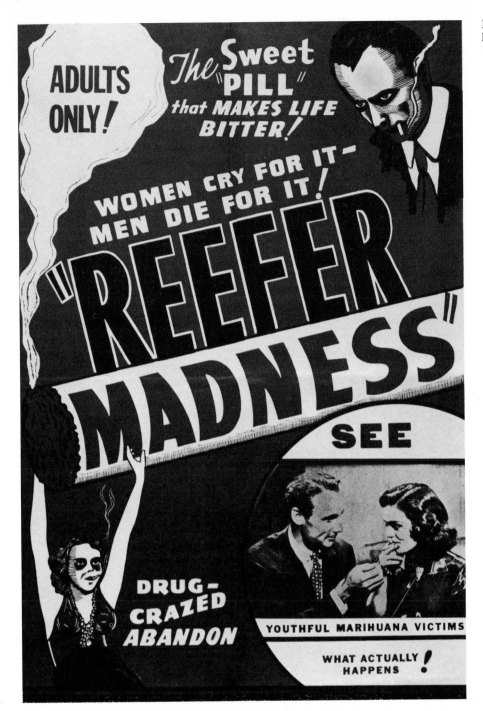

Be Warned! Reefer madness lurks to trap the unwary in the 1939 exploitation classic.

an analyst, she emerges a reformed character, helping a narcotics agent (Lyle Talbot) to track down slimy heavy Alan Baxter.

Mention of Lyle Talbot brings us to a minor digression, a brief excursion down one of the more bizarre byways of the exploitation movie. In the early 30s Lyle had been a jaunty Monogram leading man; he had rubbed shoulders with Lupe Velez in *Mexican Spitfire's Elephant* and starred in Paramount's 1939 *Parole Fixer* as a jut-jawed G-Man. Ten years later, and running to fat, he had fallen on harder times. Hard enough to involve him a film produced by that shadowy figure of legend, Edward Wood Jnr. Edward Wood Jnr, film maker, pornographer and transvestite, inhabited the seventh circle of Hollywood's poverty row. A husky Marine during World War II he had gone into battle wearing a bra and panties under his battle dress. As a director of grade Z horror films — *Plan 9 from Outer Space, Bride of the Monster* — he cut a dashing figure in high heel shoes and female pantsuit. With this kind of background it was hardly surprising that Wood leapt at the chance to cash in on the sensational Christine Jorgensen sex-change trial of 1953. The result, *Glen or Glenda?* is one of the great curiosities of cinema.

The film opens with the suicide of a transvestite. Cut to a bleak poverty row 'office' set in which a psychiatrist (Timothy Farrell) is deep in conference with burly policy chief Lyle Talbot. The former hard-bitten G-Man and scourge of the mobsters is now 'desperate' to prevent another tragedy. But as happily married Glen cruises the women's lingerie stores and dallies with his wife's angora sweaters, it looks as if another heartbreak is on the way. While all this is going on there are frequent interruptions during which we are treated to the sight of a haggard Bela Lugosi slumped in the gloom of a study festively decorated with skeletons, stuffed crocodiles and bubbling test tubes and intoning such helpful snippets of wisdom as, 'Pull the string! Pull the string! Life has begun! A story must be told!'; or, more pertinently, 'You are society, judge ye not!'; and finally, amid montages of atom blasts and thundering herds of buffalo, 'Beware of the big green dragon that sits on your doorstep! He eats little boys! Puppy dog tails! Big fat snails!' All this had little to do with cross-dresser Glen's overpowering desire to slip into his wife's panties, but the down-and-out Lugosi was an old friend of Wood, and at $400 he came cheap.

At last the anguished Glen confronts his wife with the dreadful truth. 'I don't fully understand this' she pluckily remarks, 'but maybe together we can work it out', handing Glen the prized fluffy angora sweater he has always craved. 'Should I let him wear women's clothes or should I put my foot down?' she agonizes. Only time will tell.

This pleasant diversion has carried us some way from the theme of 'wild youth', a recurring Hollywood motif since William Wellman's *Wild Boys of the Road*. The 40s saw a number of films which dealt with young people caught between innocence and experience and suffering the consequences. Among them were *Youth Run Wild* (1944), a characteristically intelligent B from Val Lewton's RKO unit directed by Mark Robson; the 1945 *They Are Guilty* (parents, of course, with the long suffering Lyle Talbot involved again); *Accent on Crime* (1946); and the 1949 *City Across the River*, with Tony Curtis in a small role.

In these films the blame for juvenile delinquency was laid at the door of neglectful parents or explained in terms of bad environment (in the style of *Dead End Kids*) or wartime social upheaval. In the 50s it was a youth culture itself which was identified by 'concerned' adults as the cause of all the trouble and frequently described in the hysterical terms of the 1957 paperback 'Teenage Jungle':'Here is a frightful indictment of youthful crime and vice in the USA. It shows how the violent and sex-crazed teenage cult exists in a living nightmare of ruthlessness and depravity. These are the ordinary kids you read about every day of your life — ordinary, that is, until they shoot a storekeeper, assault a girl, torture a bum or wind up dead in a ditch.' This overheated outpouring sounds just like a promo copyline for such AIP Classics as *Motorcycle Gang* or *Hot Car Girl* and in fact provides a neat reflection of the attitudes of the Hollywood operators who cashed in on the nation's apparent alarm at teenage gang wars, clashes between dragsters and bikers, and rumbling away in the background, the demon rock 'n' roll.

'Cash in' are, indeed, the *mots justes*, as the teen culture itself was in great measure the result of a postwar consumerism which was adroitly manipulated by a gang of middle-aged entrepreneurs — 'Colonel' Tom Parker, Albert Zugsmith, Alan Freed — a process brilliantly caricatured in Frank Tashlin's cynical, garish *The Girl Can't Help It*. The icons borne aloft into the explosion of teenpix which followed Sam Katzman's *Rock Around*

Juvenile hood Tony Curtis (left) lurks in the background next to Richard Jaeckel in *City Across the River* (1949), an anaemic version of Irving Shulman's novel *The Amboy Dukes* directed by Maxwell Shane.

Clean young America. Lee Kinsolving and Patty McCormick in Buzz Kulik's *The Explosive Generation* (1961). More like a damp squib actually, with high school teacher William Shatner precipitating an uproar when he tries to introduce sex into the curriculum.

An echo of *Dead End:* John Cassavetes, Mark Rydell and Sal Mineo are teenage hoodlums in Don Siegel's *Crime in the Streets* (1956).

179

the Clock in 1956 were those of Marlon Brando in Laslo Benedek's *The Wild One* (1953) and James Dean in Nicholas Ray's *Rebel Without a Cause* (1955). These A features were firmly rooted in the old Hollywood 'problem' picture tradition but nevertheless contained two performances which provided touchstones for all the subsequent low-budget biker heavies and mixed-up high school kids. The shades of James Dean even stalk through *I Was a Teenage Werewolf.*

If rock 'n' roll represented a universal youth currency, then its chief Hollywood broker was Sam Katzman, veteran producer of *Spooks Run Wild* and *Captain Video.* Sam's pioneering *Rock Around the Clock,* directed by B wizard Fred Sears, with Bill Haley and the Comets, the Platters and Freddie Bell and the Bellhops, set the pattern for all subsequent rock exploiters. Sam had a keen ear for the latest musical fad, and the skill to turn it into a rush-released feature which would hit the drive-ins at the height of its popularity. With *Rock Around the Clock,* Katzman achieved the rarely realized aim of all exploiters, its instant assimilation into the culture from which it sprang. If live rock 'n' roll provoked frenzies of teenage violence, or at least newspaper reports about violence, then so apparently did Sam's film. In Britain, after ritual seatslashing in several cinemas, a number of town watch committees banned the film. The ensuing uproar and free publicity must have been music to Sam's ears. By the end of 1956 Katzman had ground out an equally successful follow-up, *Don't Knock the Rock.* Five years later as Chubby Checker's *Let's Twist Again* hit the top of the charts, Sam swooped to sign the new star for and instant film. It's title, naturally, was *Twist Around the Clock,* and that of the sequel, hard on its heels, was *Don't Knock the Twist.*

The plots in these films are of surpassing flimsiness, merely an excuse to jam together as many headline acts as possible within the space of eighty minutes. *Go, Johnny, Go* produced by Alan Freed, is hung around the efforts of America's favourite DJ to save orphan Jimmy Clanton from a life of crime and transform him into crooner Johnny Melody. With Freed orchestrating events in a style that contrives to be both strident and ingratiating, there is a halt every ten minutes for a musical number, some of them preserving on celluloid acts of considerable interest for researchers into the more arcane reaches of 50s rock. There are interminable sets by black novelty groups like the Cadillacs and the Pink Flamingoes, whose specialities, in between the doo-wops, are hair-raising splits and funny walks that would do credit to John Cleese, though they also recall the great tap-dancing routines of such legendary figures as Chuck and Chuckles. The amazing Ritchie Valens warbles 'Ooh, My Head' in a cafe called Henry's Hideaway, but is left singing alone as Freed and his entourage rush off on another hairbrained scheme. Drape-jacketed Eddie Cochrane, still a revered figure in Britain, sings 'Teenage Heaven', and in a strange after-hours jam session in Henry's Hideaway, Chuck Berry snakes his way through 'Little Queenie', with Freed contributing a zomboid performance on drums that makes Dave Clark look like Buddy Rich.

Go, Johnny, Go inhabits a frantic world of teen consumerism, shamelessly manipulated by Freed and old-style Tin Pan Alley types, in which the kids even have to pay to participate in their publicity stunts. The links with straight showbiz are brought home during the Flamingoes' act, played out in front of a draped curtain and huge Grecian urns choc-a-bloc with plastic flowers. Freed spends a lot of his time hanging out with a middle-aged balding PR man who looks as if he started out plugging songs for Al Jolson. It's amusing to watch them uneasily rubbing shoulders with Chuck Berry, who rather improbably seems to be Freed's chief confidant. Barely suppressing a leer throughout, he adds a pleasantly subversive tone to the programmed mediocrity surrounding him. Just as in *Don't Knock the Rock,* the aim is to demonstrate that rock 'n' roll is a 'harmless outlet for today's youth'. Accordingly Freed provides a fantasy land in which Mom and Dad can pop down to the Krazy Koffee Kup to see just what it is that makes the youngsters tick. The silly old fools can even dig the music, provided it is watered down by the likes of Jimmy Cavallo and the House Rockers (complete with accordion), and stir themselves into a stiff-jointed jive. The cynical assumption is that it is possible to manufacture a star — and no one could be more processed than the weasel-like Clanton in his shiny Italian suit — and foist him on the squealing, hand-jiving teen masses.

The ultimate crass identification of rock and Middle America comes in a moment of pure kitsch in Freed's *Rock Rock, Rock,* in which a perfectly hideous child in a frilly frock shrieks out 'Baby Wants to Rock' on a country club patio surrounded by a group of grinning idiots in white tuxedos. The film also features 13-year-old Tuesday Weld (with voice dubbed by Connie Francis) in an archetypal lather of the pubescent agony in which these films revelled. Tuesday spends the entire film worrying about the effect arch-rival Gloria's blue strapless evening dress will have on Teddy Randazzo at the High School Prom. Appearing amongst long-forgotten groups like Cirino and the Bowties is little Frankie Lymon (13 going on 35) reminding us in arch style that 'I'm Not a Juvenile Delinquent.'

Juvenile delinquency was kept firmly in the background in musical teen films and their non-musical 'mild youth' equivalents, although the hero might be pressed into a scrap to defend his manhood. In *Rock, Pretty Baby,* aspiring saxophonist John Saxon loses his cool at a party when girlfriend Luanna Patten turns up with a local wolf, and the resulting free-for-all leaves his parent's house in a shambles. But the movie concludes happily with his combo securing an engagement at a summer camp run by the Order of Bisons.

In *Untamed Youth* (1957) Lori Nelson and Mamie Van Doren, hitchhiking to Hollywood, are picked up on a vagrancy rap and get thirty days remedial on a cotton farm. This outfit is run by a lantern-jawed psychopath (John Russel) who feeds his snarling Dobermans steak and gives the kids the dog food. Dotted around the landscape are various reminders of paranoid America — paunchy sheriffs in the pockets of local fat cats and leathery cowpokes out of their heads on cheap Muscatel and just itching to beat up on a rock 'n' roller. Things go from bad to worse. Five-months-pregnant Baby Jane collapses and dies in the cotton fields, and then the kids discover that Russel is planning to smuggle in sweated Mexican labour to undercut his rivals. They stage a mutiny, cotton-pickin' Eddie Cochrane is enrolled as a temporary deputy and Russel and his henchmen are rounded up. At regular intervals Mamie wiggles her way through a number of impromptu rock numbers in the canteen (she's a fledgling singer) but it's a sign of Hollywood's deep confusion that the final sequences show her doing a Carmen Miranda routine on a TV show, busily unzipping bananas by the dozen, surrounded by a gang of chorus boys in straw hats and flared culottes.

The cycle was sputtering to an end in 1965 when *Swinging Summer* was released. A band of survivors from earlier teenpix stage a series of summer concerts at Lake Tahoe. It's twelve months since *A Hard Day's Night,* but these elderly teenagers (most of them look well over 30) seem locked in a time warp: the leading men are all astronaut look-alikes and the women heavy-chested Barbie Dolls wearing a weird assortment of leisure wear, including polo neck bikini tops, which are a lasting tribute to man-made fibres. Hero Rick (William Wellman Jnr) is continually snapping out earnest one-liners like, 'Hey, it's conference time, kids', as the big night approaches when, for some inexplicable reason, the Righteous Brothers, Gary Lewis and the Playboys and 'Mr Personality' Donny Brooks are due to appear before the polyester-clad hordes. There is a 'chicken run' on water skis, Raquel Welch playing a bespectacled blue-stocking forever quoting Freud by way of the Reader's Digest, and a gang of incompetent hoods brought in by a jealous lifeguard to break up the kids' fun. The director's obsession with wiggling bottoms and crotches pays off in full at the end when Raquel Welch tosses aside her specs and leaps on the stage to belt out 'Ready to Groove!'

For sex, drugs and all the mindless violence that go with them, one has to turn to AIP, Albert Zugsmith and exploitation producer Joe Solomon's Fanfare. 'Wild youth' storylines were just as formula-bound — heroine loves impulsive but generous-spirited hero but is also attracted to the sleazy leather-jacketed, reefer-toking heavy. In AIP's *Motorcycle Gang* (1957) Anne Neyland is torn between nice young Steve Terrell and bad guy John Ashley; Fay Spain has the same problem in *Dragstrip Girl* (1957). In 'concerned' films, like Don Siegel's *Crime in the Streets* (1956), nasty gang leader John Cassavetes is given a degree of psychological underpinning, but in the main the bad guys are just there because they're there. The most compulsively watchable delinquent of them all was Richard Bakalyan, rapping out the jive talk and pushing junk to the kids in *Hot Car Girl* and *The Cool and the Crazy* (both 1958).

In Albert Zugsmith's minor masterpiece *High School Confidential* (1958) narcotics agent Russ Tamblyn uses more subtle methods, enrolling as a student in order to break up a drugs ring. In a bizarre touch he stays with his 'aunt', the divine Mamie Van Doren, who is squeezed into a clinging sweater several sizes too small for her and looking for all the world as if she has been shot in the back by a couple of cruise missiles. 'Don't tell me you never rode in a hot rod or had a late date in the balcony?' she coos at an uptight teacher.

In Europe there were a few attempts to provide carbon copies of 'wild youth' films. The German *Teenage Wolfpack* (1957) starring Horst Buchholz, succeeds despite its rather odd dubbed soundtrack. The British *Teenage Bad Girl* of the same year, a superior production directed by Herbert Wilcox with Anna Neagle, Sylvia Sims and Kenneth Haig, was kept alive by good performances from the principals. Over *Beat Girl* (1960), starring teen idol Adam Faith, it is best to draw a discreet veil. Despite trying hard, none of these films could match the offhand punk elegance which characterized cheapies like Roger Corman's *Teenage Doll* (1957), at the end of which a female gang, 'The Black Widows', march defiantly into the headlights of waiting police cars.

One minor genre the British sensibly chose to leave to Hollywood, and specifically to director William Asher, was the beach party movie. Bognor Regis, alas, provides no substitute for Malibu. According to Asher (director of *Beach Party, Muscle Beach Party, Bikini Beach, Beach Blanket Bingo* and *How to Stuff a Wild Bikini*) the antiseptic antics of Frankie Avalon, Annette Funicello, and assorted beach-bunnies and surf-jockeys, were a response to America's desire for 'clean sex' and the growing lack of interest in juvenile delinquency. They were also a recipe for complete boredom. Even a relatively undistinguished 'wild youth' exploiter like *Dragstrip Riot* boasted a 'chicken run' on the railroad tracks and a psychotic bike gang leader who seemed just a little more than naturally fond of his chief lieutenant (he gives a marvellous sub-Brando display of choked-back grief when the henchman hurtles to his doom off a mountain road). In *Bikini Beach* the climax is a pie-throwing marathon in a 'beatnik' cafe, and the menacing bikers are dealt with by middle-aged Robert Cummings. By the mid-60s, when Jan and Dean had been blown off their surfboards by the advent of the Beatles, the beach party was over, and with it a ten-year cycle of teen exploitation films which, if nothing else, provided a delirious sociology of American youth in the years between Korea and Vietnam.

above left
Dick Miller as 'Shorty' in Roger Corman's rock 'n' roll exploiter *Rock All Night* (1957). After an openening clip of The Platters, the rest of the film is located in a virtually deserted bar whose hapless patrons are subjected to alternate doses of execrable music from the house band, the Blockbusters, and the homicidal threats of a couple of hoods who hold the customers hostage.

above
Jerry Lee Lewis pounds out the title song in the sensational opening to Albert Zugsmith's *High School Confidential* (1958).

left
Lori Nelson looks 'real gone' as she strums away while sister Mamie Van Doren struts her stuff in the cotton farm bunkhouse in Howard W. Koch's *Untamed Youth* (1957).

183

above
Anne Neyland and Steve
Terrell in *Motorcycle Gang*
(1957) directed by B veteran
Edward L. Cahn.

Wistful British biker, Rita
Tushingham in Sidney J. Furie's
The Leather Boys (1963).

June Kenny gets set to go out in
Roger Corman's *Teenage Doll*
(1957).

184

High school heartthrob Teddy Randazzo and 13-year-old Tuesday Weld (playing 18) fibrillating with teen torment in *Rock, Rock, Rock* (1956). Weld's vocal efforts in this film were dubbed by Connie Francis.

Cirino and the Bowties conduct an impromptu dandruff inspection in *Rock, Rock, Rock*.

below
Adam Faith is knocked out by coffee bar queen Noelle Adam in the British *Beat Girl* (1960). Slouching subsersively on the left is moody young Oliver Reed.

left
This hot combo from *Rock, Pretty Baby* (1956) features Rod McKuen on bass, John Saxon on saxophone and Sal Mineo on drums.

right
Hello sailor. Jack Nicholson takes a beating in Joe Solomon's *Hell's Angels on Wheels* (1969) directed by Richard Rush.

left
Chubby Checker, looking remarkably like Mohammed Ali, in *Don't Knock the Twist,* a Sam Katzman epic of 1961.

far left
Gonks Go Beat, a strange British offshoot of the Beatles industry of the early 60s.

right
The Great Stoneface (Buster Keaton) in *How to Stuff a Wild Bikini* (1965).

right
Rock 'n' Roll High School (1979) directed by Allan Arkush, an amusing pastiche of the teenage exploitation movie produced by Roger Corman. P. J. Soles (centre) and her friends exercise in the gym in time to the Ramones' title song.

AND NOW THE STARS

The Bs have their own iconography, both ancient and modern, stretching all the way from George Zucco and Toby Wing to Dick Miller and Candy Rialson. Low budget films have always thrived on the reassuring familiarity of the actors whose distinct personas and often narrow acting ranges fit snugly into the limited spectrum dictated by rudimentary scripts and tight schedules. Serving as a kind of visual shorthand, they allowed hard-pressed directors to dispense with sheets of dialogue. It was only half-jokingly that Phil Karlson remarked of his days at Monogram, 'If I had one guy that had to go to the bathroom, I was in trouble.' When working on *The Great Impersonation*, Evelyn Ankers found herself being hustled by director John Rawlins into a love scene with Ralph Bellamy without even the formality of an introduction.

Nowhere was the quality of instant recognition more heavily bestowed than on the B heavies: heavy-lidded Luther Adler; paunchy William Conrad; twitchy Elisha Cook Jnr, forever replaying his role in *The Maltese Falcon*; smooth John Sutton; thin-lipped George Macready, compulsively collecting knives in *My Name Is Julia Ross*; John Carradine mad-doctoring his way through such stomach-churning rubbish as *The Astro Zombies*; J. Carrol Naish, taking on everything from an escaped convict in *King of Alcatraz* to a comic French waiter with a neat line in Micky Finns in *Good Morning, Judge*.

Character players had the advantage of being able to move easily from Bs to As. George Zucco was a star on the PRC lot in Z-grade horror quickies like *The Feathered Serpent*, but slid down into supporting roles in *The Seventh Cross* and *Madame Bovary*. Life could be frustrating for talented performers like Chester Morris and Louise Allbritton, jealously confined to the treadmill of the second feature by bigger names several rungs higher up the studio ladder.

The big stars all had their B mirror images. Clark Gable look-alike John Carroll played 'the King's' role in *Congo Maisie* (1939), a B remake of *Red Dust* and the first in the Maisie series. Dane Clark never shrugged off his image as a poor man's John Garfield. At Universal Gloria Jean was a second string Deanna Durbin. At Fox John Payne had to make do with the scripts rejected by Tyrone Power. Warners even tried out troupers Dennis Morgan and Jack Carson in a pale imitation of the Hope and Crosby 'road' films in the short Two Guys series, but *Two Guys from Milwaukee* failed to strike the same chord as *Road to Morocco*.

Other stalwarts of the Bs stuck fast in the Great Grimpen Mire of the second feature for no other reason than they were just not good enough to

go any farther. The thespian talents of the likes of Tom Neal and Ann Savage were undeniably limited, but occasionally a director such as Edgar Ulmer was able to exploit this one-dimensionality within his own bleak inner vision. These qualities, or rather lack of them, rang equally true in the 50s science fiction trash like *Attack of the Fifty Foot Woman* or *Invisible Invaders*, full of zomboid performances from Allison Hayes, William Hudson and John Agar.

Occasionally a B spear carrier was given the chance of a leading role. Not all of them were as fortunate as Boris Karloff, who seized his part in James Whale's *Frankenstein* with the fierce certainty of a man who recognized a once-in-a-lifetime break. Nevertheless, the demands of the B production line could on occasion give bit-part players like Steven Geray – a familiar 40s face in small foreign roles - an unexpected spell in the limelight. Joseph H. Lewis coaxed a fine performance from Geray in *So Dark The Night* (1946), but the Hungarian actor slipped back again into his accustomed character slot, memorably in *Gilda*. Perhaps it is to Steven Geray and to all the other contract players with familiar faces but less familiar names that this book should be dedicated.

Two actors guaranteed to add their distinctive lustre to any film in which they starred. Vera Hruba Ralston and Forrest Tucker join forces in Republic's *Jubilee Trail* (1954) directed by Joseph Kane. Ralston, a former Czech skating champion who always had considerable difficulty in handling dialogue, had the good fortune to be the wife of the studio's boss, Herbert Yates. Try as he might, however, Yates could not foist her on an unwilling public and the husky, slow-speaking leading lady never became a star. Here she met her match in Forrest Tucker, whose truculent style graced a number of 50s British Bs.

above
Chester Morris, a B leading man of great charm, particularly in the Boston Blackie series, who later in his career went on to success on the stage and television.

top right
Rugged Jack Holt as he appeared in the 1925 *Wanderers of the Wasteland.* The dependable lead of many an action B of the 30s, he also did serial duty as Holt of the Secret Service.

right
Preston Foster, a dependable lead of the 30s, poses with canine friend. Foster is the one in the cap.

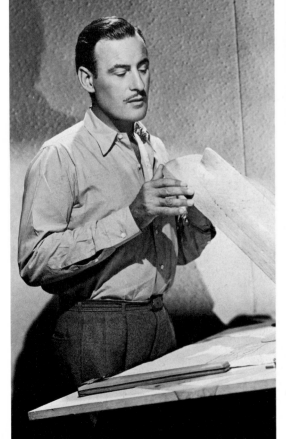

top left
More doggies. Robert Armstrong, whose one really big role was the blustering film producer Carl Denham in *King Kong,* takes a stroll in his Hollywood home with his Scotty Filthy McNasty.

above
Another smoothie, Warren William, svelte impersonator of gentleman detective Michael Lanyard (The Lone Wolf) in a successful Columbia series, the first of which was the 1933 *Lone Wolf's Spy Hunt.*

left
Suave Tom Conway, George Sanders' brother and star of The Falcon detective series, takes time off from filming to pursue his hobby of boat designing. Sadly the bottle was Conway's undoing. After sliding into obscurity in the 50s, he briefly reappeared in 1967 as a destitute alcoholic. He died the same year.

191

above
Richard Arlen became a star in the 1927 *Wings*, but in the following decade he came to earth as the lead in a string of B thrillers. Eventually he found a comfortable berth with the Pine-Thomas team, starring in many of their outdoor actioners of the 40s and early 50s.

above right
Silky-smooth villain George Zucco was a star on the PRC backlot in low-budget horror films like the 1942 *Mad Monster* but slid well down the cast list in more prestigious productions like *The Seventh Cross*.

right
John Sutton, an English character actor who specialized in swashbuckling villains, looking rather ill at ease with a brown derby jammed on his head.

Like Richard Arlen, silent star Richard Dix found his vehicles declining in the 30s. Nevertheless, his career ended with a flourish in The Whistler series, the first of which, *The Whistler,* was directed by William Castle in 1944.

George Macready exuding wickedness from every pore in *The Bandit of Sherwood Forest* (1946). A descendant of the Victorian tragedian Macready and one of cinema's greatest heavies, he is best remembered for his role as Rita Hayworth's husband in *Gilda.*

above
Rondo Hatton, whose deformities (the result of acromegaly) earned him a brief, pathetic career in horror films of the 40s. They included *The Pearl of Death* (1944), *Spider Woman Strikes Back* (1946) and *The Brute Man* (1946).

above right
Elisha Cook Jnr in the 1940 *Tin Pan Alley*. In the same year he played Wilmer, the twitchy little gunsel in *The Maltese Falcon*, a performance which led to a lifetime's work as cowardly neurotics. His most memorable B version of Wilmer was as Lawrence Tierney's accomplice in Robert Wise's *Born to Kill* (1947).

right
English character actor Lionel Atwill in one of his best roles as the one-armed police chief in *Son of Frankenstein* (1939). An accomplished mad doctor, he turned Lon Chaney into a high-voltage menace to society in Chaney's first Universal horror film *Man-Made Monster* (1941).

above left
Leon Errol in the 1945 *Mama Loves Papa.* An Australian comedian who came to films via Broadway musicals and vaudeville, his talents were wasted in a string of 30s two-reelers and 40s comedies like *Gals Incorporated* (1944) and *Hat Check Honey* (1944). However, he did provide an admirable foil for Lupe Velez in the Mexican Spitfire series, playing the dual role of Uncle Matt and the stuffy British aristocrat Lord Epping.

left
Frankie Darro (right), the boyish star of an entertaining Monogram detective series of the early 40s.

above
Sonny Tufts in 1943 at the height of his brief success following Paramount's *So Proudly We Hail.* From then on Sonny took a well-lubricated downhill slide via *Cat Women of the Moon* (1954) to *Cottonpickin' Chickenpicker* (1967).

above
Rod Cameron, the rugged star of a host of B actioners, who started his career as a stand-in for Fred MacMurray.

above right
Jock Mahoney, who changed his name from the more exotic Jacques O'Mahoney, worked his way up from Columbia serials (*Roar of the Iron Horse*, *Gunfighters of the Northwest*) to star as Tarzan in a number of low-budgeters of the late 50s and early 60s.

right
Another Tarzan. Bruce Bennett, a long way from the days when, as Herman Brix, he starred in the 1935 serial *The New Adventures of Tarzan*. He changed his name in 1940.

left
Trench-coated Maxwell Reed, the brooding lead in a number of forgotten British B thrillers of the 50s.

below left
Steve Reeves actually displaying a few signs of life as he takes time off from flexing his pectorals to drain a goblet of Samian wine in Jacques Tourneur's *The Giant of Marathon* (1960).

below
Lyle Talbot, a veteran of the Bs who somehow managed to survive a featured role in *Plan 9 From Outer Space*. Here he appears in a late-50s television feature, *Chinatown Squad*, in which he starred opposite Valerie Hobson.

Vivacious Gale Storm touches up the biggest Easter egg in Hollywood which, for reasons best known to the studio's publicity department, is parked on her front lawn. Sons Peter and Phillip participate in these strange 1947 proceedings.

below

Lovely Jane Frazee, who lent talent and charm to a number of B musicals of the 40s. She was memorably paired with Joan Davis in the 1944 *Beautiful But Broke.*

Jane Frazee's co-star in *Beautiful But Broke,* Joan Davis, mugging away in a studio publicity shot. A veteran of vaudeville, Davis was expert at wringing laughs from the weariest of routines.

above
Ann Savage wearing one of
Carmen Miranda's cast-offs in
Two Senoritas from Chicago,
directed by Frank Woodruff in
1943. She is ensured a tiny niche
in cinema history for her role as
Vera in Edgar Ulmer's *Detour*
(1946), one of the best, and
cheapest, Bs of the 40s.

left
Toby Wing, a cut-price Jean
Harlow of the 1930s.

left
Mamie Van Doren in 1954, the year of her screen debut in *Forbidden*, already displaying the charms that led to her memorable appearances in Albert Zugsmith's schlock classics *High School Confidential* and *Sex Kittens Go to College*.

far right
Veda Ann Borg, a familiar face in second features of the 40s, including minor classics *Isle of Forgotten Sins* (Edgar Ulmer, 1943), *Revenge of the Zombies* (Steve Sekely, 1944) and *Forgotten Women* (William Beaudine, 1949). Here she is all kitted up for Gregory Ratoff's *Irish Eyes Are Smiling* (1944).

right
Louise Allbritton, the Carole Lombard of the second feature, an accomplished comedienne who never broke free of the B tag.

right
Frances Gifford, star of Republic's 1941 serial *Jungle Girl*, trained as a lawyer before finding a career in Hollywood.

far left
British actress Evelyn Ankers came to Hollywood in 1940 and quickly became the queen of the Universal B unit, screaming her way through innumerable horror second features. She is married to actor Richard Denning.

left
Gloria Warren, as she appeared in *Cinderella Swings It* (1943).

Chic Lupe Velez, explosive star of the Mexican Spitfire series. She was married to Johnny Weissmuller between 1933 and 1938. She committed suicide in 1944.

Lori Nelson, who played sexpot Mamie Van Doren's nice sister in *Untamed Youth* (1957) and exercised a strange fascination for Jack Arnold's Gill-Man in *Revenge of the Creature* (1955). Like many starlets she got her chance in a series, the Ma and Pa Kettle films of the early 50s.

Two fifties floozies.

above left
Marie Windsor, the '60 cent special' who as the Camerons remarked looked 'like Loretta Young with touches of Edmond O'Brien'. She was superb as an undercover cop masquerading as a gangster's hard-bitten widow in Richard Fleischer's *The Narrow Margin* (1952).

above right
The 'animated waxwork' Mari Blanchard. In the Audie Murphy version of *Destry* (1954) she played the Marlene Dietrich role. She was spotted for films in a bubble bath photograph.

And finally, in characteristically ebullient form, the Gill-Man in *Revenge of the Creature*.

BIBLIOGRAPHY

INDEX

Page numbers in italics refer to illustrations.

Books

Barbour, Alan G., *Cliffhangers — A Pictorial History of the Motion Picture Serial.* A & W, 1977.

Barbour, Alan G., *A Thousand and One Delights.* New York, 1971.

Baxter, John, *Science Fiction in the Cinema.* Tantivy, 1970.

Belton, John, *The Hollywood Professionals,* vol. 3 (*re* Edgar Ulmer). Tantivy, 1974.

British Film Institute, Dossier No. 7, *Roger Corman's New World.* 1981.

Cameron, I. and E., *Broads.* Studio Vista, 1970.

Clarens, Carlos, *Horror Movies.* Putnam, 1967.

Everson, William K., *The Detective in Film.* Citadel Press, 1972.

Gifford, Denis, *A Pictorial History of Horror Movies.* Hamlyn, 1973.

Koszarski, Richard (Ed.), *Hollywood Directors 1941-76.* O.U.P., 1977.

McCarthy, Tod and Flynn, Charles, *Kings of the Bs.* Dutton, 1975.

McClelland, Doug, *The Golden Age of B Movies.* Charter House, 1978.

Miller, Don, *The Hollywood Corral.* Popular Library, 1976.

Stallings, Penny, *Flesh and Fantasy.* Macdonald and Jane's, 1978.

Strauss, David F. and Worth, Fred, *Hollywood Trivia.* Warner Books, 1981.

Warren, Val, *Lost Lands, Mythical Kingdoms, Unknown Worlds.* Simon and Schuster, 1979.

Film Review, Macdonald, 1944-1954.

Magazines

Cine Fan, nos. 1 and 2.
Cinema (*re* Joseph H. Lewis). Fall, 1971.
Film Comment ('World of Gods and Monsters; The Films of Larry Cohen'), Sept./Oct., 1978.
Mad Movies, Cine Fantastique, no. 13.